CURSEANOVA

The Unprecedented Times of a 2,080-Week-Old Baby

© Copyright 2021 by Jamie Greenlees All Rights Reserved

TABLE OF CONTENTS

CHAPTER 1 – THE BOY WITH NO BRAIN

From the moment I left my dad's ball sack, I knew that my life was going to be crowded with extreme upset, misery, and sin. I'm also sure that if my Dad invented a time machine, he would go back to the night I was conceived and put a condom on. That may seem potentially a negative comment to make, however I am one of these people who rather than say "you only live once, so make the most of it", would say "from the moment you are born, you begin dying". These are just some of the light hearted and soul warming thoughts I am about to embark on throughout this epic read, therefore I would suggest putting your seatbelt on, and prepare yourself for the ultimate train journey to 'upbeat central', calling at 'feelgood park', 'High-spirit lane', and 'Happy-go-lucky boulevard'. This train has also been cancelled due to a passenger being murdered at 'Satan street'. Hi, I'm Jamie, sometimes referred to as Curseanova, and welcome to my story.

I do not remember my first two years of life, as I was just a small bundle of apocalyptic joy that had not developed enough brain power to register and record thoughts, in-between all the being sick and crying. If only a major event would sweep the Universe and imprison everybody inside our own home's decades later, I'd have the time to think about and write about said thoughts, oh wait! Undoubtedly, I was without question inventing an ultra-green energy source to prevent global warming for future generations or envisaging what I would spend my spacious amounts of money on when I became either an International porn star, or an open-heart surgeon. As I cannot remember the very beginning of my life, I will skip to when I was 24 months old. Before I do so, I would just like to add, that people who describe their baby as 18 months old are pinheads. Your baby is one and a half. ONE AND A HALF! I wouldn't announce to my friends in the pub that I am 479 months old and weigh 7.26035182 x 10(13) nanograms. NO!

I'd say "Hello, I'm Jamie, and I'm a vivacious alcoholic that is ballooning in size every time any human breathes air. Who fancies 25 kebabs and an enormous bag of Twiglets?". If you are looking for a happy ending to this book, for example I meet my Princess and live happy ever after, or I become a Premiership footballer that makes lots of money and fame, then I would urge you to think again. In fact, rip this book up or throw your kindle out the window. A lady kisses a few frogs to meet her Prince, but the women I meet sleep with the whole pond, and I don't play football because I am afraid that somebody will eat my kebabs and Twiglets if I put them down.

At the ripe young age of 24 months, I captured my first memorable glimpse of life. It was a giraffe juggling revved chainsaws whilst riding a motorbike at top speed. With this being my primary vision since birth, I could only assume that this was basic normality. It wasn't until I was about 30 years old, that I was informed by my parole officer that it was certainly not, and I quote, 'the norm'. So, there I was in my cot, having a cheeky wee on the sheets, and absorbing the sounds of harrowingly screaming, when the giraffe suddenly appeared riding around my bedroom. I thought it was my Mum, but then again, I didn't know what a Mum was, or have any language, but I was quietly confident that I didn't have a six-foot neck or an off-orange shade of skin. From recollection, my next memorable vision was a few days later, and was the most disturbing of them all, and still haunts me to this day. It was Cilla Black singing on the TV. I had repeat nightmares for weeks about her coming around to my house and tickling me. It was awful. I'd lay awake in hot sweats clutching my teddy called 'Charlie microwave', looking like I'd just had a bath with my clothes on, and then gripping my tiny hands tightly around the cot wood.

Even at such a young age, my intellect was vastly above extremely high. This came in handy for many reasons. Firstly, when ever my Mum was watching television, and my dad was asleep on the sofa, I would crawl to the door, then run into the kitchen, drink a bottle of whiskey, run back to the living room door, then crawl up to my dad, to put the empty bottle in his hand, and casually crawl around the carpet with Charlie. When my parents we're in bed, I'd often open all the cereal boxes and bags of crisps like a normal child, so it would appear a wild monkey had broken in during the night. Being able to walk without showing anybody meant I could be monumentally lazy and still be chauffeured around in a buggy. My Dad was often in hospital because my Mum would beat him up for drinking so much Whiskey, so I was usually a bit tipsy in the buggy when Mum pushed me to his ward each week. I knew I had to walk soon, as my parents would become suspicious if they still manoeuvred a shopping trolley around Tesco's with me in the baby seat aged 2,080 weeks. The only other occasion to which I used my secret walking skills, was when my next-door neighbour would play his drum kit in the early hours of the morning, and I'd climb out of the bedroom window, run to his front door, crawl through the cat flap, and stab him in the eyes with cocktail sticks. On one occasion I violently inserted a drum stick up his rear end. The second reason my abnormally advanced intelligence came in useful, was because I passed my driving test aged two and a half, ie not 30 months. Not many babies have legitimately passed their driving test prior to being able to walk. I should have got a medal or knighthood, but I didn't want to make a fuss. We often hear of so called 'miracles' that happened before our time, such as turning water into wine, and parting the red sea etc, nevertheless I had created my own modern day sorcery by driving a Camper Van at maximum speed through a supermarket window on my third birthday, all because I got bored of my crayons.

Once it was finally established that I could walk, my life progressed smoothly according to God's evil plan. On my third birthday I was sliding down the staircase rail at home to save time getting to my birthday presents, and flew off the end, intern smashing my skull into a metal ornament of a tiny aboriginal man holding a gigantic razor-sharp sphere. I spent my third birthday having stitches in the back of my head, but on the plus side, I did get the bed next to my Dad, who was laying there in agony with a neck brace on, due to Mum catching him drinking all the Whiskey again. That really cheered me up. I wrote 'cock' around his neck when he went into a mild coma. It was hilarious. Mum brought my presents to the ward, and I got a magic 8 ball. I shook the ball and asked, "Will I be happy in life", and it produced a 'ha' pyramid face up in the bubbly water. I did however make a friend in my ward. He was another 3-year-old boy, who was in for drinking a litre of paint for a bet and his heart nearly exploded.

The boy was called 'Billy Lightswitch'. I'd never forget him. He was one crazy wild card. I didn't see him again until I was 4 years old, and with Billy being a gambler, I bet him a bag of pickled onion monster munch crisps that he wouldn't saw his own legs off, but silly Billy stepped directly up to the plate, and recorded the limb removing stunt on his parents camcorder to document it. The video got seven views when it was uploaded to the internet two decades later. Being in a hospital made Billy a little happier once the regret had kicked in, and winning the crisps was a bonus. A few weeks later, Billy almost died when he fell down the back of a radiator trying to retrieve a 50p coin. He got stuck and was almost centrally heated to his own demise. Don't panic, he recovered, and appears more in this book as we grew up together. I just wanted to make it transparent from the outset that he lived to see another day. Still, enough about that jerk, lets talk endlessly about me.

Drawing back to my comments of previous concerning me finding my Princess, I met my first serious girlfriend at play school when I was three and a half (assuredly not 42 months) old. She was beautiful, with long blonde hair, had her own teeth, and a 'My little Pony' pencil case. Her name was Nicola. We hit it off straight away when playing on the slide, and she didn't even know I was blind drunk. Nicola was hard work, and not the easiest girl to convince to sleep with me in exchange for a blackcurrant Ribena. I had to box clever to get her attention as more than just a friend, so I made her an artistic collage of cute hamsters with axe's in their backs, using discarded cigarette butts and a Pritt Stick. She LOVED it. When I handed over the article, she immediately thought that I painted something noticeably better than the Mona Lisa and threw me to the ground for a proper snog with tongues and everything.

Although we were both only three years of age, we checked out which mortgage deals were available, so that we could runaway together and get our own love pad. We didn't have any money apart from our piggy banks of loose change, so we would have to have found dirt cheap accommodation to gain homeowner status, and do things ourselves, like steal food, and cut each others hair. Nicola lived near me, so sometimes when our Mum's got together, I would see her, and we would make bombs in my room using a junior chemistry kit I acquired, and then blow up cars in the street. We started with my annoying neighbour that plays the drums all night. Besides being super bright for such a young mind, I was also extremely intuitive, so I siphoned off some of our new home savings to a separate piggy bank for when Nicola and I had a child, as no doubt in the years to come, our kid would be relentlessly plagued on social media (if it was invented by then) with friends commenting on their family photos 'I cannot believe how sexy your dad is' and would therefore require therapy sessions to get over it, so they would be financially ready.

On the days that I didn't see Nicola, I would listen to 'Ray Parker Jr - Ghostbusters' on vinyl at full volume until my Mum eventually curled up in the corner next to the fridge/freezer and started crying again. I would still think about Nicola, but then I'd get a raging erection which I had to hang out the window until it went down ten feet. My Mum would give me a bath and then read me a nice bed time story. A few chapters from 'A Clockwork Orange' or the obituaries in the 'Basildon Recorder' usually sent me to sleep overjoyed. A boy at play school said his Mum read him about 'Roger red hat', which was a stupid book for sane children. Basically, he was a stick man called Roger, who had a red hat, and would run around the garden smelling flowers, or helping old ladies cross the road. Roger even had a friend called 'Billy blue hat' who performed equally as dull activities that crumbled the entire brain of children.

Approaching my fourth birthday, Nicola and I had been officially a couple for almost 6 months. We hadn't had sex yet, as we wanted to wait until we were both five. After all, you can't rush true love. We had only encountered one major argument, to which she said, "I'm leaving you because you never give me any space", to which I replied, "wait up, I'll come with you". Nicola then threw a steel Tonka truck at my head and knocked me unconscious, and I was mature enough to forgive her but not stupid enough to trust her again. To celebrate our anniversary, I set fire to her Barbie dolls and was sick in her back pack. She got me a nice watch. I truly loved Nicola, but there was another boy hanging around her like a bad smell. It was 'Billy Lightswitch' from the hospital. I was infinitely jealous, and told the Police he was a rapist, but sadly he was never arrested, as the short arm of the law weren't interested in what was deemed to be a minor offence. Every day that went by, Billy became closer and closer to Nicola. Billy told her exactly what she wanted to hear, like "you don't smell like death", and "I love your moustache'", etc. It was I that told Billy whenever a girl asks a boy for his opinion, she didn't really want his opinion, she just wanted her own opinion repeated. On the result of my sound advice, Billy took Nicola on a date to the roundabout in our local park and shared a Capri Sun together.

I spent that evening telling a piece of cheese how bad my life was when Mum went up the hospital to visit Dad after his latest drinking injury that I had gotten him into. I decided to ask Nicola to marry me, so I zoomed into the closest cemetery, dug up the first women's grave I could find, removed the wedding ring from her metacarpal, and headed to Nicola's house dressed as a scary clown. I will never forget Nicola's Dad answering the door and kicking me square in the penis. Nicola was watching 'Button Moon' with Billy, so that made me even more irate, because it was my favourite TV programme. I sat in-between the two of them and turned to Nicola. "I love you all with my demons, will you marry me?" I asked. The blood rushed from her face, and my little red nose fell off, but before she could answer, Billy twatted me with a video case. Anyway, long story short, she said no, and I left the room to wash Billy's blood off my hands, after I'd run him over in a sit-down lawnmower, then launched him over the garden fence, to enjoy a friendly savage attack at the neighbour's Alligator farm.

CHAPTER 2 – TCP BREATH

At the age of four, and still coming to terms with the fact that Nicola and I were no longer a couple, I was delighted to learn that My Mum was pregnant with my baby sister. I couldn't wait for her to be born so that I could bully her, however it turned out that I would really love her, and would be the perfect big brother, and always look out for her. When Mum went into labour, I went to see her for a bit on the way to see Dad in the next ward. Mum had cut off Dad's left ear off for drinking so much Whiskey again. I think she intuitively gave the idea to the film makers of 'Reservoir Dogs', which had not yet been invented.

I played 'Connect 4' for a few hours whilst Mum was in the delivery room. Little 'Lola' was born safe and well, and I now had a little sister. This was also the year I started Primary school, and my odyssey into life really started to take formation. My first teacher was called 'Mrs Curtain-rail' who looked like a serial killer, but she had a heart of gold, and was by the far the loveliest teacher I could have wished for. I recalled one instance when she caught me injecting a deadly substance into a fellow pupil but didn't tell my parents. This was a good result for me, however she bred into forgetfulness by proceeding to slip up on parents evening by saying "Jamie is great with his nine times table, but he shouldn't inject poison into Daniel Warrington's buttocks during class". I got into a heap trouble that evening for being great at my nine times table. Never again would I absorb mathematical data and emphasise my power to be nurtured too easily. Everyone knew that learning things was bad for you. We also had a class photo that day, and I wet my pants beforehand, so I had to wear emergency clothes from the potent lost property basket. My fellow pupils we're all smartly dressed in their little uniforms, and I was perched on the end in a summer dress with egg mayonnaise stained down the front. I literally wanted to die, but sadly, I lived.

As my first year of Primary school developed, Mrs Curtain-rail paired pupils off to work on a special project to write a poem. I was hoping to be paired with Nicola, but instead I received the short straw and was budded up with Billy. The task in hand was to write a creative poem about school and our friends. I had this in the bag, because I wrote limericks for the Daily Mail when I was two years old and would make Billy look like a mindless amateur. Nicola was paired with Daniel Warrington, who had returned to school after a recent brush with death. As I put pen to paper, the words oozed out of me, and continued to flow with ease line after line, thus completing the exhibit in no time. I told Billy I was the best for making it happen so spritely, so that he could go and stamp on ants in the playground, when really, I would be stitching him up with my poem, like the friend I was. Once everybody had written their master pieces, we took turns to stand up and recite our poems to the rest of the class. Nicola and Daniel did a lame speech about how the dinner ladies were nice and 'Hop Scotch'. It was painfully monotonous. I subtly named mine 'Romeo and Nicola'. The original full title was 'Romeo aka Jamie and Nicola and I hope Billy Lightswitch dies', but I was told this rubric was potentially offensive. I stood at the front of the class clasping my poem and unleashed an excellence of words....

"Nicola should be with Jamie,
If not, she should go to jail,
I hope Billy Lightswitch falls out of a conker tree,
Head first onto hundreds of upright nails."

Mrs Curtain-rail applauded the main event and requested that the Head Master immediately offered me a teaching role at the school and a thousand pounds worth of football stickers and sweets. The Head Master automatically agreed and realising my impending wealth and fame, asked for my signature on his forehead and back. Billy was outraged, because I think he detected the underlying meaning of the poem. Nicola on the other hand realised that I was destined to become famous and came to the front of the class for a tirade of long passionate kisses with me, but then sat back down next to Daniel Warrington, and started rubbing his privates with a 2B pencil. If I were to be with Nicola, she would arrive hand in hand with her flirty problems. If I were to meet somebody I liked, I was adult enough to appreciate she would arrive with some baggage, but I simply wasn't prepared to settle for a cargo ship of pandemonium. Upon reflection, I should have written my second choice poem about the UK only having four habitable weeks per annum, what with two of those weeks being in Spring when it's still nice out, a bit leafy, but not many wasps about, and two weeks in Autumn when in remained acceptable out, and there were no longer any wasps. The rest of the year was either boiling, freezing, or wasp raves. This was my first meaningful experience of believing that the more romantic you are, the further away it gets you from the one you love. I wasn't too disheartened, because 'Roxanne Beachballhead' came up to me, and said that she loved the poem. By the way, this is where I introduce Roxanne to my story. I hadn't spoken to Roxanne before, because her breath smelt of TCP, but then I simultaneously wanted to kiss and marry her after such kind words with reference to my poem. A voice in my head whispered, 'give her a few wheelbarrows full of extra strong mints and a reduction to the size of her head, and that will be the only serious work she needs for you to be able to love her properly'.

That night I tattooed Roxanne's name on my nose using fountain pen ink and a soldiering iron. Mum went ballistic, so I told her that Billy Lightswitch did it because he got jealous that I had more head lice than him. Mum believed anything I told her. Such a div. Once I told her there was a spelling mistake on page 54 of the kettle's instruction manual. She didn't even check the validity of my claim. Anyway, school became awkward after the tattoo incident, especially when it came to love interests, and meeting somebody different also called Roxanne Beachballhead.

On my fourth birthday, Mum arranged a party for me at our

house, and hired a magician. He was the type of guy that got sacked from working in a petrol station for reassembling a sex attacker and had limited employment options. When he arrived at the house with his magic wand and deck of cards, I soaked him with a water pistol that had acid in it. My new baby sister was in her room sleeping, and Mum stayed downstairs with me and my school friends, to check that the magician didn't touch any of us inappropriately. The magician called for a volunteer, and Billy Lightswitch stood up. He was invited to select a card from the pack, but I was hoping the magician would ask him to climb into the box, and then a horrendous accident would take place whereby he got sawed in half. No such luck. I did suggest the magician blindfold himself, strapped Billy to a revolving wheel, drank a drum of vodka, then throw knives at him. Even in the 1980's, it was still tricky to get that level of family entertainment signed off by employers.

I was however elated that Roxanne came to my party, and we smoked copious amounts of mega hard drugs in the garden together whilst she questioned me about my tattoo. Dad had discharged himself from hospital, because Mum had told him about my tattoo, and turned up half way into the magician's act to rollock me. I was high, so I wasn't bothered. It certainly was a birthday to remember, because when my Dad collapsed next to the shed, I put a bear trap around Billy Lightswitch's ankle to force him into a River dance. My sister was awoken by the sound of the ambulance, and the magician left early with psychological trauma. It was gruesome, so I think it was probably the best birthday ever.

A few weeks later Roxanne dumped me, all because I put dead wasps in her pencil case. Some people just can't take a joke. I knew then that Roxanne and I were not compatible, after all I was a Capricorn, and she was a slut. She was laughably childish about the whole thing and kept harping on about how I needed to grow up. I then had to sit next to her in assembly, so when we had to sing 'all things bright and beautiful', I purposely wet myself and then quickly cuddled her. Nobody dumps me without a valid reason! Mrs Curtain-rail told me off, and I went home that afternoon crying. This is the part where you stop reading for a second and make lots of sympathetic noises for me. I really liked Roxanne. I got on my BMX and rode to the local sweet shop. It was only once I grabbed a bag of fizzy cola bottles that I realised I was naked. You could get away with doing that back in the 80's, but not in 2021 at the age of thirty-nine, as I can assure you from first-hand experience, due to lack of selfie likes on social media and unsolicited visits to my house from people in the medical profession. Next paragraph please.

Entering the second year of Primary school, I had put Nicola and Roxanne down to bad luck and looked forward to a new term with my new teacher 'Mrs Earwax'. The school year started with a class trip to the National History Museum. I was hung-over, boarded the school coach with the rest of the class, and I sat next to the new girl 'Anna Plug'. Anna had been living in London, but her Mum had relocated to Essex with her, due an unfortunate case of mistaken identity involving her Dad, a gun, an innocent drug dealer, a trigger pulling circumstance, her Dad's fingerprints, and an unsuspicious death, leading to her Dad being put in prison. To this day nobody knows what happened. Upon arrival at the museum, I fashioned a twelve-foot ladder made of paperclips and mounted the fossil of a T-Rex. I felt so cool, however security took a dim view on my stunt, and rapidly ejected me from the museum. I spent the remainder of the day languishing on the coach and flushing fellow pupil's personal belongings down the on-board toilet out of boredom. Anna came back to the coach and we shared a tuna sandwich together after all the sex. It was so romantic. We couldn't wash our hands after, because almost everything that wasn't nailed down was in the toilet. I was beginning to fall for Anna after only one morning, so I thought I'd tell her that I love her in a roundabout way. "Fancy a bath?" I said. "Oh, erm, yeah ok, maybe later in the week" she replied. Anna was quivering with excitement. Love or lust, she wanted a date in the bath with me. She was blue hot with anticipation as to what other sensible delights I had up my sleeve for her.

Unfortunately, the time came when the others returned to the coach. The steaming bag of dung Billy Lightswitch surged on first and right behind him was Nicola. I stared Billy out, and they sat down together all smug and happy. A few seconds later, Roxanne Beachballhead and Daniel Warrington followed behind them hand in hand. My entire love life had been rescued from the sewer and regurgitated a few feet away from me, and I had to endure them gloating away, like they had just stuck their arm up inside a vending machine and retrieved that difficult bag of crisps jammed between the revolving arm and the glass front. I was a good job that I only had two hobbies, being making daisy chains and domestic violence, because my skills in one of those areas was about to became overwhelmingly beneficial.

My saving grace was that I had a bath date with Anna, so when the coach driver pulled into a lay-by to see why the toilet had flooded, it felt like the right time to propose. "Anna Plug, we've known each other for almost a day, will you marry me?". The jubilation was too much for her, and after a long awkward silence and many legalities to overcome if she wanted to, Anna put down her cigarette and said, "I can't believe you didn't ask sooner and yes of course I will". I'd never been so happy before, even though she'd probably leave me for an electronic jar opener once they'd been invented, as that's all men were ever useful for. I swam up and down the coach naked, then set off some fireworks I'd forgotten about in my back pack. The odour from the toilet was unbearable, but nothing else mattered at this moment in time, apart from getting married to my fiancé called Anna whilst having Roxanne Beachballhead printed permanently on my nose.

As soon as I got home, I told my Mum that I was getting married. "That's so cute, but you have to be 16 years old to marry my darling" she said. "I don't care, I am marrying Anna Plug, and if you, or the Police try to stop me, I'll take your Freddie Mercury cassette tapes, and mangle them all up" I replied. My adult response from a supposed child stunned my Mum, and she walked over to the telephone to call Anna's Mum. I still don't know how my Mum knew Anna Plug's Mum, her name, or her phone number, but at least it was being dealt with, and I assumed Mum was calling her about the dress rehearsals or the seating plan for our big day.

"Hello is Liz Plug there please?" my Mum said.
"Who?" the lady on the other end of the phone replied.
"Liz Plug please. It's Jamie's Mum speaking".
"Madam this is the child abuse hotline!".

So, my Mum didn't know Anna's Mum, and she must have hit redial by mistake and got through to the last number I had called for a desperately senior prank. Nicola came around to congratulate me on my engagement, but I was sick of her adultery, and force fed her some expired corn beef. Nobody likes expired corn beef. Nicola had used me for my intelligence so that she could have three-month holidays four times a year when I rich, as I wasn't having it. She went away upset but not hungry, and I started to arrange my wedding plans. I considered holding the reception at McDonalds but thought it may have been a bit too mainstream.

Ideas circulated inside my over developed brain all evening, and eventually settled on the local Charity shop, because it was easy to break in to, and they closed at lunch times. My life was as organised as the bargain bin at Woolworths, and picking the best location was becoming a horror show. In the end, my problems were solved when I spotted Anna sharing a bag of aniseed balls with Harry Mushroom from the year above at the bus stop. I couldn't be dealing with another messy break up, so I prayed to God to take pity on my soul and wash away my sins by calling off the engagement. Billy Lightswitch told me that they held hands as well, and that made me feel wholly sure I had made the right decision to void our impending wedding. Anna said, "we need to talk", but whenever girls say that to a man, it's never about football. I advised her I had nothing further to listen to. I was a huge fan of holding hands in public, but not with any filthy immoral cheat. To compensate for the lack of hand holding with Anna, I decided to partially heat a jacket potato in the oven, then cupped it in my left palm. I looked seriously cool strolling into class with a warm jacket potato in my hand, which felt like I was holding somebody else's hand, and with the added benefits of knowing I had something to eat later, and it wasn't going to cheat on me or talk all the way through a film I as heavily invested in.

Advancing a few years to the age of 9, because nothing really happened until then, I decided to runaway from home. I had many reasons to runaway from home, but the main one was that my Mum had confiscated my Sega Mega Drive for burning our house down. She was often pedantic like that at times. I was livid. One night when Mum went to visit Dad in hospital, and I told my sister Lola that I was going to a school disco. I picked up my tent and duvet and promised her that I would be back in a couple of hours. I gave her a cuddle and plonked her down in-front of Eastenders with a box of pork scratchings. She was engrossed, and I slipped out the front door. After about seventeen or eighteen steps, possibly nineteen, (I can't remember really as I wasn't counting), it began to pour down with rain, so I pitched my tent at the end of my road, as it was too wet and windy to make it to the nature reserve on my school's ground. The sole reason I was heading to my school's nature reserve was because my new teacher 'Mr Buttwitch' had built a wooden hut next to a pond in the centre of it. He was a crazy man with an out of control beard that housed many species of wildlife. One pupil swore blind they spotted a zebra in Mr Buttwitch's beard once. I think he built the hut because his wife left him, and after an amicable divorce, his ex-wife got to keep their house, and he was left with the glassware. He was also obsessed with Wombles and got his outdoor inspiration from the programme. He was a freaky outcast in total honesty. My tent was pitched, and as I attempted to zip up the canvas, I saw the snake Daniel Warrington and Roxanne heading up the street. As they got closer, I yanked the zip on the tent so hard to close the door, that it broke, and Daniel stood there laughing. I may have been having a bad tent day, but he was having a bad face life, so I was still winning.

It was too wet and cold to fight him, so I stayed calm, and plotted a flawless and doom riddled revenge from the confines of my canvas tent. I was shocked that Roxanne ignored me, but I had bigger fish to fry when I lit the barbecue stove inside the tent with too much lighter fluid, and it was burned to high heaven. It's not every year you burn down two homes. A nosey neighbour called the fire brigade, so I legged it into the bushes and curled up next to a dead fox. I forced myself asleep and dreamed about Superman accidentally dropping Lois Lane and Jet from Gladiators mid-flight over Bowers Gifford leading to them land naked either side of me, but then I woke up drenched alone. Tough times.

After an hour of bone chilling lightning and maggots from the fox slithering up my Reebok Classics, I decided to return home. Mum was still not back, and Lola was writing 'please help' over all the walls with a spray can, because she saw somebody on Eastenders do it earlier. I threw the tent into the garden, washed the burnt skin off my arms, and got into bed. It was a shocking day to be fair. I woke up in the morning and Mum was scrubbing Lola's graffiti off the walls. Now remember I said I would always look out for my sister? Well here is a prime example of how I did so. Mum stormed to Lola and I and yelled "who sprayed all over the walls?". Lola and I stood petrified on the outskirts of the living room unsure how to respond. Mum followed up with "was it a burglar?". Lola then thought she was in the clear, until I replied, "no it was Lola".

Back at school, it was fast approaching Christmas, and Mr Butt-witch asked us all to make a list of things we wanted from Santa that year, whilst frantically removing butterflies and lions from his beard. I wrote down in bold that I wanted a skateboard or a self-sufficient off grid log cabin in Alaska. I added the Argos catalogue number of every skateboard to a piece of paper, as my daft old mother bought me an encyclopaedia and socks the year previous. Just because I loved my Mum, it didn't mean I had to like her too. Billy Lightswitch got a remote-control car last year, and I threw my Encyclopaedia at it when I pointed up at the sky and said "Look, a submarine". He still didn't know it was me, but he had an inkling. If I got a skateboard and he broke it, there was never any doubt that I would have roundhouse kicked him in the throat until his head became detached from his body. My parents were not exactly swimming in money, not just because Dad was always in hospital with mysterious injuries, but Mum had been slogging away working long hours at a care home, to ensure Lola and I always had food on the table. This aside, I firmly believed that money could not buy happiness, unless of course it was used to purchase a skateboard or Champagne. After all, you never see any unhappy people drinking Champagne whilst skateboarding on an expensive Yacht. That would be outrageous.

CHAPTER 3 – DINNER LADY KIDNAP

On Christmas day, my Nan and Granddad came around for a Turkey roast, and I eagerly awaited their presents, so that they would leave quicker. Granddad arrived in his John Virgo waistcoat, and Nan ploughed straight through to the Kitchen without saying a word to get knee deep in Christmas wine. She was a woman after my own heart. Granddad dished out the presents, and Nan passed out with her head in the washing machine. I think she got that tip from me. Mum got gold earrings, Lola got an Etch a sketch, and I got a slapped wrist for finishing off Nan's wine. The Turkey had been in the oven far too long, so we had carrots, runner beans, and ice cream. If KFC wasn't shut on Christmas day, I'd have been hammering on the door waiting for them to open and securing a bargain bucket of chicken.

Nan got a second wind and started break dancing on the kitchen table whilst we were eating and cranked up Madonna's 'Vogue' for some mid dinner karaoke. Her Zimmer frame wheels splashed into my ice cream. I was enraged. Mum didn't seem too impressed and gathered up some leftovers to take to Dad in hospital. Granddad tried his finest to coax Nan down from the table with a barrel of Bombay Sapphire, and she glassed him with a broken wine bottle, but the timing could not have been better in view of Mum about to head up to the hospital. I was left with Lola and Nan, so the fun could begin. Nan had a few more pints of wine, and abducted next doors cat. This is the same cat that I found but ran away then came back again before going missing. Nan was royally inebriated by now and started to apply eye shadow and lipstick on the cat. Whilst that kept Nan occupied, I let Lola play on my new Skateboard, and I went upstairs to peer out the window and into my neighbour's garden to watch her sunbathing topless. It was a very warm Christmas. The attractive lady next door always knew when I was relieving myself as she would often catch me twist the blinds for a few minutes, and when I'd finished, I'd twist them closed again. I picked up my tissues and turned around to find my Nan just standing there, arms folded, and looking cross. Maybe she was a pervert.

I went outside to join Lola and we saw Nicola and Billy Lightswitch riding their new bikes. I stopped directly in front of them and ate twelve stocked handfuls of stinging nettles, then skated off into a parked car. That gave Nicola something to think about. I could tell that the nature of my gesture had torn her between myself and Billy, and when I jumped off the pavement and over a dozen vertically stacked dust bins on top of a crane, and landed perfectly back on the skateboard, she knew that she had made a brutal mistake choosing Billy over me. She immediately became so unwell upon realising her mistake that vomited up her back bone. Nicola turned to Billy and said, "were finished", and I rocketed over to her at top speed. We attempted to kiss, but my mouth was buzzing from the stinging nettles, and Nicola couldn't stand up on the account of having no spine. Billy stood there with his hands over his silly ugly face and cried ferociously to dehydration. Nicola spotted the opportunity to come to my house with Lola and witness my Nan grill me again about the Roxanne tattoo on my nose, which bizarrely she had not noticed earlier, and the other issue of what she had witnessed when my neighbour was sun bathing. Nicola produced some emergency pop corn from her 'I love Jamie' engraved purse I bought her and followed us back to the house for the premiere of me getting told off.

My last year at Primary school was the apex of all my schooling years. Aged eleven, my school arranged a trip to Wales for an adventure week of super fun activities, such as abseiling, wind surfing, archery, murder, and quad biking. It was a mixed trip for the boys and the girls, however genders were genders back then, and we were separated when it came to sleeping arrangements, which was a sore shame for those who were romantically linked, and for those hoping to find extra activities that were not on the pre-approved list. There were approximately twenty-five of us that participated in the trip, and the whole event was total carnage from beginning to end. The first sign of trouble was when the coach stopped at a service station on route to Wales, and my friend Sam Flip-flop took a photo of all the boys on a 35mm disposable camera. Crazy times. This all seems very innocent, but he then got naked and threw bricks at the coach driver because he was partly excited and mostly mental.

He smeared Oil of Ulay all over his chest and body slammed the driver as he came out of a coffee shop. One of the teachers called Sam's parents, and advised that he had been given a verbal warning for his behaviour. For unknown reasons, my friends and I had an unprecedented desire to get naked all the time, and there never any reason to question it back then, so we'll move on swiftly accordingly. When we arrived at the activity centre, I helped Nicola with her suitcase off the coach, the boys went to their sleeping quarters, and the girls to theirs. There were roughly 12 boys in my dormitory, and rapidly learned that on the other side of our adjoining wall was a group of girls from another school. This was good news. I set up a stall outside their window offering full snogs for 50p and a queue formed that was visible from space. Crazy Sam banged on the wall so hard with a fire extinguisher to get their attention, that he smashed the solid metal object directly through the wafer-thin wall, creating a giant hole between two bunk beds, and he stole all their sweets and mini bra's.

Sam Flip-flop was drunk and repositioned two of our bunk beds to cover the huge gap in the wall, but the girls on the other side alerted their snooty teachers, and before we knew it, Sam was escorted back to England. I remember reading about the extreme dangers of drinking and smashing fire extinguishers through walls, so that was it for me, no reading ever again. With a gaping hole in the wall and eleven boys in the dormitory, we created a civil riot in honour of Sam. Billy Lightswitch kicked off the fun by picking his nose and wiping it around the hole in the wall, but then Andrew Doorhandle (the oddest pupil in our year) went into the staff room, kidnapped a dinner lady, and shaved a Nazi sign into her back. That scene was a bit rich for me, even by my standards. I was gutted that Sam that gone home, as he was a good friend, so you could always guarantee a decent bout of laugher and violence when he was around. Andrew was a mate, but I could have done without the whole kidnapping and racism thing. The owner of the centre was called 'Baloo', and he was also a nice guy, so we helped plaster the hole in the wall and went into girls' room that had grassed on us, and shaved their hair off, then emptied tins of dog food into their suitcases. We then proceeded to hold them hostage until they signed a confession in blood that Sam had nothing to do with the redecoration of the wall in question.

With day one out the way, we indulged in various activities on day two, starting with abseiling and wind surfing. I did a joint abseil with Nicola, and we kissed half way down in front of Billy Light-switch in a bid to ruin his life and lead him to killing himself. Roxanne said to me "mature Jamie. Very mature", so it was evident she was going to be getting a deadly tarantula released into her sleeping bag that night. After a day of vigorous activities, and the group all in high spirits, we went to the activity centre disco. This included our school, and the other school that reported Sam for making a hole in the wall. They looked like posh aliens with no hair. That'll teach them to mess with an angry boy with clippers. As soon as 'The Shamen Ebeneezer Goode' came on through the speakers, a war erupted on the dance floor. The boys from the other school knew about the wall incident and started circling the boys from our school. Andrew Doorhandle was the first to retaliate by pushing one of the lads against the tuck shop door. Soon the whole rekus emanated, and there was a mass dual between the schools before the lead singer of the band Mr C could finish his rap and 'Salt n Peppa' came on. I turned on the smoke machine, then extremely efficiently forged, laminated, and planted a fake ID on all the boys from the other school, confirming they were in a secret gang that blows up activity centres. I notified the relevant authorities, and within a matter of seconds they descended into the activity centre from helicopters.

Mr Buttwitch and one of the female teachers separated the schools, but the contest was not over. Insane Andrew placed a giant sock over his head, assembled a group of six strong and fired a water cannon into the other boy's room when the clock struck midnight. I felt sorry for the guy. I had my issues, but Andrew was four stops beyond clinical. That night he broke out of the activity centre with a pint of semi skimmed milk and a syringe, then injected said milk back into a cow's udder, because he felt that milk men were the sole cause of destroying the Planet. The next day our school attended archery lessons. Giving disobedient ten and eleven-year-old children the ability to fire sharp arrows at 150mph was never going to end well. The instructors placed balloons on the bull's eye targets, and the plan was for pupils to fire an arrow into the balloons, with the aim of popping them. It sounds so amicable. An eleven-year-old with a gargantuan bow and long acute arrow firing from ten feet at a balloon. What could possibly go wrong? Well, it transpires, 'quite a lot' was the answer. As I lined up my first arrow with the target, I noticed Billy Lightswitch pull down his pants out the corner of my eye and he started making sheep noises. Without a moment's hesitation, I pulled back the arrow, amended my direction of sight, and fired the fibre glass missile directly into his scrotum. Allow me to confirm to you for free, that It was a blood bath. One of the assistants ran for the first aid box, but Billy had already lost 3 pints of claret by the time the assistant had left the target board. I didn't know whether to laugh or cry, but I knew I wanted to laugh, so pretended to cry, but secretly laughed. Billy lay wounded on the ground in unimaginable pain, so whilst Roxanne tried applying pressure to his leg; I casually kicked him in the face and filled his ears with mud. In addition, being fully aware of his hay fever, I aggressively smeared freshly cut grass in his eyes. If Nicola hadn't have held me back by promising to buy me a video cassette tape of my choice, I might well have urinated up Billy's nostrils too. The take home message here, is that I was mere pup, young and immature, and never pull your pants down around a jealous eleven-year-old rival holding a weapon. I should rephrase that, but I'm sure you get the point. The coach journey back to the activity centre was very uneventful, unless you class getting a blow out on the front tyres of the coach, and careering off the Severn bridge into the river, intern killing the driver.

Safely back in England, and back at school, pupils were asked to write a poem about our trip. Prior to this, there was some tricky paperwork to complete concerning the hole in the wall, the disco riot, the child archery hospitalisation, and the coach murder. The emphasis for my poem was loosely based on a song that myself and some of the others had written and chanted on the coach between activities and before the driver died. If I remember correctly, it went as follows:

"I saw a bird, with a yellow bill, it landed on, my window sill, I coaxed it in, with some chicken chow mien, stuck a straw up its nose, and sucked out its brain"

Maniac Andrew and I memorised the lyrics, and adopted our own approach to the lyrics, then screamed them into Daniel Warrington's face whilst he was trying to play Tetris on his Gameboy with Anna Plug. If I remember correctly, it went as follows:

"I saw a cock, with a very red face, he had an attack, when I sprayed him with mace, it was Daniel Warrington, who is a bag of malodorous poo, tell anyone about this, and I'll end you"

Once I had returned from the two-day suspension, there were only a few more days left of primary school, and I firmly believed that some of the kids were getting emotional. Many children hate school, and for the most negative person since that time an aeroplane came through my bathroom window when I was cleaning my teeth, or the world began, I was really going to miss primary school. We threw basketballs from distance at all the single glazed assembly hall windows in celebration, and then cut each other with army knives and the broken window glass. One boy got aids, but fortunately he was going to a different secondary school. Nicola suddenly became best friends with Leah Slug, because she was going to the same secondary school as her, but I was going to be stuck with maniac Andrew and a few others. Lightswitch, Warrington, and Beachballhead were going to one school, Myself, Plug, and Mental Andrew were going to another. Would I see Nicola again? Would I make new friends with Roxanne Beachballhead written on my nose? The prospect of having lost her forever became un-unnervingly real. I was sick in my mouth but swallowed it to save face. Nicola and Leah Slug became inseparable. Leah was hot and my type of girl, as she was unpredictable and fracas. She could invite you out to dinner, then at the click of a button, set you on fire, roll you up delicately in carpet, throw you off a cliff, and meet you at the bottom to behead you. That's how I knew we were a strong match, but she had blue eyes, and I couldn't deal with that negativity in my life.

With emotions running high, and the last day of Primary school upon us, a day of high jinks soon got under way. A boy in our year named Graeme Dishwasher, kicked off the proceedings by attaching portable speakers to his cassette Walkman and blasting '2 Unlimited - No Limit' into the playground, whilst playing the usual 'launch a basketball at the single glazed assembly hall windows' game. Windows smashed all over the school, and some used the broken glass to construct weapons for a new game called 'Murder in the light'. Dishwasher was so hard he could beat people up with his ears and therefore nobody ever questioned his actions. He told me that his Granddad invented wasps, so I just said," that's cool". I overheard him tell Anna Plug that he ate red hot coals from a BBQ set, and his head blew off like a space shuttle, but then had his face reconstructed to the exact mirror double of Bruce Willis. Whilst those stories are believable, he slipped up on one occasion, by confirming that when he cooks pasta, instead of draining the shells with a sieve when cooked, he would empty the saucepan onto his already capped hands, and then wait for the boiling water to seep through his fingers. He told everyone that only he could do this because he was so hard and had hands made of asbestos, yet when I made the point, he would need three hands to pour the saucepan onto his already cupped hands, he went berserk and threw an overhead projector at me. Luckily, I used my advanced reflex ninja moves to protect myself and ended up slicing the machine into several layers using an assortment of mid-air black belt kicks. Mr Buttwitch treated our final day like any other day by hiding in the nature reserve to indulge in a few cans of dangerously cheap high yet percentage lager and a cigarette before registration. Everybody else in our year was throwing paper, bricks, and tables at each other, awaiting their last day to commence.

When Mr Buttwitch swayed back to the class room, he stated "as today is your last in this school, I would encourage you do whatever you want". It was all too surreal for me to comprehend. We all noted that Mr Buttwitch was clutching a transparent carrier bag full of lager, and that his day was booked out for that, so we did our own thing. We put raw eggs into an incubator and tried to grow chicks and a homunculus. We climbed over the perimeter fence and ran down the busy motorway naked. Some children went even more frenzied, by making glittery cards for the teachers, to say thank them for their knowledge and education. There we're some deadbeat losers in my year. Meanwhile fires tore through the school, some kids had passed out, and Graeme Dishwasher hired a bull dozer and drilled half a mile into the ground to create a sinkhole. When the final bell rang to end our last day, everybody said goodbye to those that were conscious, and I had an immeasurable nine-minute open mouth tongue snog with Nicola. Then I placed her in the recovery position and hurtled to the shop to buy her nice things. I didn't buy her chocolate, flowers, and oversized teddy bears, as she would know I was only after one thing, so I stole her an expensive bracelet to show I was serious about her. Primary school was over. Completely over. Well, almost over. Billy and I put our differences to one side for one moment, picked up the dead fox riddled with maggots that I'd had in my school bag for several years, and put it in Daniel's school bag. I'd love to have seen his face when he got home, because I had convinced his mum to put him up for adoption.

During the six weeks break before we set off to Secondary school, a group of us went to the cinema to see 'Jurassic Park'. Bedlam became priority of the day, as Billy Lightswitch established the days doings by drinking twenty-four cans of shandy bass and urinating over a pensioner on the bus ride there. This gross and indecent act cost us all being ejected from the bus, and intern missing the trailers before the film. Once I had handed over a second mortgage's worth of cash to fund a small carton of popcorn, and keg of sprite, I dived into the seat next to Nicola and let her share my feast. During the opening scene I asked Nicola if she would like to go for a romantic McDonalds after the film. No sooner than those words had left my lips, Anna Plug whispered to Billy Lightswitch what she had heard me say, and he threw Sprite into Nicola's lap. Nicola's friend Rebecca Potato helped her wipe the fizzy drink stains off her dress, whilst I had an argument with Lightswitch. Multiple viewers of the film were heckling at us to be quiet, and we cleverly swore back at them. I articulately diffused the situation by sneaking in a full sized snooker table and challenging the crowd to a frame in exchange for strawberry laces, but security came over and escorted our group off of the premises, and Billy went home crying because I sprained his wrist, then put a pencil with a rubber on the end in his ear and told him that I had rubbed out all of his feelings for Nicola. Roxanne Beachballhead was fuming. She went into Woolworths for a limitless selection of Pic N Mix and ate as many sweets as she could before her heart gave out and collapsed into a badly positioned water feature in the town centre. Billy Lightswitch had also urinated in it earlier. That lad was uncontrollable. I watched him do it whilst I tried to impress Nicola by retraining a dog tied up outside BHS to believe its name was 'stay', then giving it a series of commands such as 'go stay' and stay go' until it went mad and ate its owner.

I spent a dedicated chunk of the six weeks holiday crab fishing at the local beach. Outside of that, I made a den under the slide in my Mum's garden, using an old blanket, and sat inside thinking about Secondary school and Pamela Anderson. It was the peak of the summer, the sun was roasting, and it speedily became unbearable in the blanket den. I couldn't think straight with regards to my blueprint for horrific revenge on Billy Lightswitch. Also, the crabs that I stole from the sea died in the heat. Although Nicola wasn't there with me at the time, I knew she was laughing. If a dog can locate the source of a sound in 6/100ths of a second, why Couldn't I? Precisely. This is my story, so that's what happened. Anyway, after being bored rigid for so long, I spruced the day up hiring two private detectives to follow each other.

CHAPTER 4 – ONLY RUN WITH SCISSORS

Secondary school got underway, and besides Anna Plug and maniac Andrew, I did not know anybody else. A girl came and sat next to me on the school bus and said hello. It terrified me. People shouldn't be allowed to speak before midday. I asked her if she was a bank statement because her eyebrows were overdrawn and then enjoyed the rest of the commute in peace. We all arrived together, and met our new tutor, a ruthless Scottish lady called Miss Smell. You can't make this stuff up. The school itself was a large building that catered for over one thousand pupils and was much larger than our tin pot Primary school.

As I glanced around at my new fellow pupils, I began to feel a little scared and intimidated by them but also placed labels on them as to what kind of person they were, even if they weren't. I was hung-over that day and was wearing sun glasses to disguise the bags under my eyes. I looked so stupid. Not just because it was raining, but also, I was wearing a fancy-dress costume of Donatello from the teenage mutant ninja turtles. Cawabunga! Plug and Doorhandle sat together on a desk of two, and Miss Smell plonked me next to a stunning girl, whose name was Lisa War. Lisa was so beautiful, with long mousey brown hair, dazzling eyes, and a cute little nervous twitch. I couldn't bring myself to speak to her as I was too scared. In addition, she couldn't hear me under the costume. I sparked up a rational conversation with Lisa by telling her all about the invisible old lady that lives in hair. She was fascinated. I kept a monitoring spreadsheet of everything Lisa said to me in case we got married and I had to paraphrase her on something later in life. Women love that kind of stuff. Nicola had immediately been forgotten in a love way, and I slowly became friends with Lisa, having implemented a secret agenda to cloud professional judgment when it came to me stealing her heart.

Besides Lisa, I made friends with some of the other lads, such as 'Wayne Trafficjam', and 'Nathaniel Feet'. They would typically hang around with 'Psycho Bob', who was a lad that illegally sold chocolate bars from his school bag and pulled a pair of scissors out on you if you didn't pay up. He looked like a scarecrow. Poor kid. But at least he was lucky enough not to born me. If you didn't have enough money to pay for your illegally sold chocolate bar, you did not ever mess with Psycho Bob.

He would have zero or less hesitation to put you in the ground with a slit throat and unmarked grave for the sake of a Toffee Crisp. My best friend in our tutor group was 'Greg Fatcheese'. He was an absolute unit. A walking army tank for want of better words. This living machine was one of the funniest people I had ever met, and although he was a massive bell-end at times, he ultimately would become my brother from another mother.

Greg eloquently responded to Miss Smell's addressal of 'Hello class', by thieving her purse and opening a fully shaken can of cherry coke in her eyes. We were all handed a homework diary, to which our Parent(s) or Guardian(s) would be required to sign each week for the next five gruesome years. The first day was a dreadful and boring tour of the school, meeting some of the teachers, and maxing out Miss Smell's credit cards at lunch time on fish and chips, and some fishing gear from a local shop. I saw Nicola on my walk home with Lightswitch, and they looked sickeningly happy. Nicola approached me and asked how my first day went, wo which I replied, 'you need to get over me as I'm with Lisa War now'. I thought I was being clever, but hurriedly realised that Nicola didn't know who Lisa was, and I looked ridiculous dressed as a Donatello.

I had my first piece of homework to complete, and it was to write a short speech about myself to recite to our tutor group later that week. I put on my thinking cap, requested to Mum that I couldn't possibly eat chips for dinner, and pressed on with my speech. Mum and Lola, we're downstairs tidying my empty tequila bottles, when suddenly there was a deafening banging at the front door. Roxanne Beachballhead's Mum had come around to see my Mum about borrowing a spice rack, and moving out of the area, but Roxanne also rocked up with her. Beachballhead was about to talk to me, so I went out and kicked a football against a wall for five hours with Trafficjam and Feet. Roxanne watched me playing football from her bedroom window, and she said I was a trillion times better and sexier than Ryan Giggs. I modestly agreed then told her to go away as my award-winning speech wasn't going to write itself.

The next day, it was time for our first P.E. lesson, which stood for 'physical education', and not 'pig entrails' in case you we're wondering. There is a big difference between running around a field before playing rounder's and presenting the teacher with a large wheelbarrow full of pig insides. Trust me! Basically, this lesson was all about the taller and faster and fitter people showing us not so slender types up. Every P.E. lesson had at least one show off, that would either sprint backwards, perform a merciless Rugby tackle on the smallest kid in the class intern leaving them with brain damage, or doing so many repetitions of press ups that our teacher had to rename them 'Earth downs'. I learned this vital intel early on, when I was running around the school field with my tutor group and tried to keep up with the lightning pace of Lisa War. She was not only beautiful, but incredibly fit. Somebody said she once ran thirty-seven marathons in one hour, and yet I got out of breath getting off the sofa to change channels on the TV.

Lisa left me for dead, and I was at the back of the pack with Greg Fatcheese having a crafty cigarette. He became a saving grace to those lessons, as he was always less fit and worse than me. Greg and I habitualy took a crate of Cider with us on our way round the field to remain hydrated before we went to the pub at lunch. Greg would sometimes pop a handful of ecstasy pills, but he was leagues above me. Once he got so high that he ran out of the school gates and was picked up by a sea plane in the middle of the Atlantic Ocean a week later. I could just about manage the grog. When

Lisa had completed her three thousand laps of the field, she waited a few months for me to finish my first lap, and then congratulated me. It was so touching that she waited to congratulate me. I told Lisa that I had an old knee injury giving me trouble, from the time I prevented a group of Terrorists from taking control of the American Embassy in London on my way to receiving a knighthood for world peace, because one of them put a Samaria sword into my left knee cap. She instantly believed me and said I was "the best".

Life at Secondary school alleviated my negative outlook on life, which felt good. The friends I had been making were much better than my previous collective of bad apples, and I awoke each morning rather excited about the prospect of school and seeing Lisa War. During the first three of my five years at school, I knuckled down with my both school and homework and embossed my authority on the school. My new positive outlook even embraced me to listen to different genres of music I had previously discounted.

I would often find myself waiting for dinner to cook, when suddenly Beethoven would come on the radio, leading me to instantaneously strip naked and do a wacky wild bokers dance, even when the owner of my local kebab shop continued to try and throw me out. It was the fourth year at Secondary school when things began to change, due to our tutor group attending different lessons with other tutor groups, integrating both people and subjects. Despite trying to be Lisa's boyfriend for three years without success, I met another good friend named Michael Hedgefund from the other half of our year. I attended both English and Science lessons with Hedgefund. By this stage in my life, I was now solid friends with Nicola, I was never going to give up on me and Lisa thing, plus I'd met a whole new load of other good eggs too. The only annoyance and noticeable physical defect I had, was my not so fashionable nose. Even if I could win Lisa over, I'd have to pressurise her into changing her name to Roxanne Beachballhead. Not many women would do that for somebody they are not into. I continued to chip away at trying to dazzle Lisa by placing suicide notes next to roadkill in order to give their families some closure, which I thought she'd find sweet. She didn't.

I even took her out for a meal and showed off by ordering every-thing in Italian, which did surprise her, but only because we were in a chinse restaurant. The last two years of Secondary school were arguably the best by far, and have so many stories to tell, so have tried to surmise the best of them, in the only way I can. Let's just say that every second of every day was a life changer for those kids when I was on school soil. That's what I tell myself anyway.

CHAPTER 5 – JACK BRUSSEL

During the fourth year at school, a geography trip took place in a town called Saffron Walden, about thirty miles from where we were based. It was a three-day trip, and unfortunately Lisa did not attend. She was too busy solely imagining me running naked on a tread mill and possibly researching how to change her name legally I imagined.

The trip itself was awesome. We arrived at a huge castle style estate, which became our accommodation for the next few days. I stayed in a room with my friend's squirrel killer 'Greg Painkiller' (not Greg Fatcheese), and a spotty guy called 'Matt H20'. Pupils were told where their rooms were located, and we all headed off to unpack. Painkiller, H20, and I, walked into the wrong room at first instance. The room we entered was plush, high class, contained three double beds, a balcony, a luxury marble bathroom, a mini bar and an ash tray. We though 'great', and I opened a beer and then jumped into the shower whilst the other two unpacked their clothes and drugs. Within minutes, Mr Brussel, our head of Geography teacher, walked in and shoulder dropped his bag to the floor in shock as to what he was witnessing. Mr Brussel had bucked teeth and was a horrid teacher that must have been bullied at school himself and had a prodigious ego. He was adamant that he was better that everything and everyone when it came to his grand stature. We called him Jack Brussel, or Sh*t Man, as he had the temper of an angry dog, and looked like one. We of course had entered the teacher's accommodation. Jack Brussel barked uncontrollably, and asked us to exit the room immediately, which I overheard from the shower. I put down my beer, dried off, and went to see what was going on. Painkiller and Matt had scarpered and left me to take Jack's final breaths of extreme temper. I waltzed out the shower with a towel around my waist and saw Jack standing there almost concussed, like he had just found out that he only had a minute left to live or been walloped over the head with a frozen chicken. I wanted to break every bone in his body, but just grabbed my clothes and scuttled out. If I had the time and the money, I would have converted the room into a roller disco and charged Jack £5 to get in once he'd correctly paraphrased the classic Rik Mayall appropriate access wording.

When I found my room, Matt and Greg were inside unpacking again, and possibly kissing a bit. "Get a room" I said in the voice of Sh*t Man to distress them. It was a small dark room with three single beds and no shower or toilet. It looked like something you'd see in a prisoner of war camp, or at the back of a field at a boot sale with a queue of people waiting to pee in. Matt went to find out where our external facilities were hiding, so Painkiller and I poured a litre of water into Matt's bed and placed the duvet on top. I then urinated into an empty coke bottle and threw it out the window, which struck the owner of the Castle on the head from our second floor. I thought I had it bad in life, but I'd never had a bottle of cloudy piss thrown at me from height, so I was one up on the owner Ruberto, who later became know as 'Noberto', because we were so clever to think of the fitting witty and grown up name.

The mini break itself was mind numbingly boring, however one aspect of one of the days was a real hoot. I still to this day cannot believe it was sanctioned, but nevertheless it happened. Groups of four pupils were dropped off in various local towns for an hour, unattended by any teacher or adult, with the objective to gain knowledge about their area in question. This was our golden ticket to bliss. Along with Painkiller and Matt, we had another lad 'Andrew Album' with us. The coach arrived at our stop named 'Thaxted', which was a small beautiful town surrounded by countryside. I jumped off the bus so quickly, that I almost broke my neck when my record bag got stuck on the wing mirror mid leap. That would not have been a great start to the day. Disabled by breakfast.

'Stevie Hairspray' and 'Sophie Valentinecard' were the two girls on our coach sitting right at the very front, and nearly died of laughter at my jump and subsequent plummet to the ground. They were clearly desperate to gain a spot on the long list of people that didn't want to sleep with me. Thaxted was so remote and rural that it only had three shops, and a small primary school that catered for a small handful of children. The four of us put our clipboards in our bags and headed directly to the closest public house. We could not get served alcohol in school uniform, so we headed to the first off licence in sight. Album looked slightly older than the rest of us, with the intermittent patches of stubble about his cheeks, so he seized the opportunity, zipped up his coat and purchased us seven crates of vodka, which was amazing, as I looked so young, I would have been asked to produce ID for an ice poll. As we slurped and guzzled away dangerously high levels of imported Russian vodka, which we re-named 'anti depressant water', we stumbled across the village lunatic. Just my luck. Every village or town has one, and it's usually me, but we were fortunate enough to meet this one with time to burn. He came up to us and did an impression of a crow by flapping his jacket and making the ear-piercing sounds. Then naturally he flashed his penis in my face, which I thought was a bit of a leap from saying "hi". Whilst the other three looked alarmed, I related to the guy in some untypical way.

We gave the lunatic a bottle of vodka from our supply, and then he climbed to the top of an old Oak tree, removed his clothes, and crouched over a sparrow nest to empty a few nuggets onto the new-borns. I knew he would. We incorporated this experience into our hour knowledge of Thaxted and placed some meat on the bones by writing down some lies, to make it seem like we had achieved something constructive. I added things like 'I met a field mouse called Rodney who was depressed about the loss of a snail', and 'the town held the World Cup in the 1700's but is a secret and only generations of families that lived there knew about'. Jack Brussel knew I was lying, but I didn't care about Sh*t man. Besides which, he couldn't disprove it anyway. He never even disbelieved the part where I said we witnessed Rod Stewart beat the living day lights out of a bus stop because he thought it called him a w*nker. We slipped a note under Jack Brussel's door later that night, advising anonymously that I knew his dirty secret about him and the History teacher Miss Cowell. This was a complete fabrication of the truth, but I wanted to make him think. I also drew a picture of a fat dog with rabies on the back of the note, with an arrow pointing to its bucked teeth that mimicked 'Jack Brussel aka you'. It was tremendously brilliant. Ok, maybe I was still a bit nasty at the age of fifteen, but I laughed all the way back to my room to find Matt drying his emergency bed sheet on the radiator. There were some other stories that didn't involve urinating on people, but I can't remember them anymore.

Back on School turf, Science and English were still my favourite lessons, as a result of the pupil re-arrangement. In Science, I was positioned on a desk with three other lads from different tutor groups. Michael Hedgefund was one of them, and two boys both names Paul. This became an eclectic mix of personalities, but one which worked effortlessly, and these friendships lasted long after school.

Michael was the easy target and used to get bullied more than me, and the two Pauls were the braun behind this outfit. The first Paul we labelled 'Boozy' in view of his alcohol stories, and the other was known as 'Bone head' as his face was largely skeleton and we weren't sure if he was alive or not. The desks in our science lessons had taller tables consisting of long work benches. This started our first gag with Hedgefund. Boozy, Bone head, and I, would remove the wood panel from in front of Michael's desk and hide his stall in there. He walked round the room trying to find it for the first few weeks until he worked out where it kept disappearing too. By this stage we had also started adding his school bag and his stationary in there, along with the corpses of pupils we had altercations with. It became known as 'Room 101', where anything of Michael's ended up. The pranks then stepped up a notch, as we filled Michaels bag with glass test tubes and Bunsen burners, so that when he picked up his back pack, a large clanging sound could be heard by the entire class, and they would all look up to see the rubber hose from a Bunsen burner hanging out of his zip. The one on his bag that was. We weren't that good. I showed Lisa War some magnesium I stole from the science lab, and she was immediately dripping wet for me. I was good looking and a thief, what more could she want? She dived at me, and we began planning our future together.

One day Bone head spilled life destroying acids all over Michael's desk, and Boozy dropped a lit Bunsen burner on top of them. The desk went up in flames, and poor Hedgefund burned his eye brows off. How we all laughed at nearly giving our friend third degree burns and eternal loss of sight. We were terrible when we all got together. The only stunt we ever got into trouble for was when our pensioner teacher Mr Gnome, that looked like a gnome, because he was a gnome, was breeding some rare species of plant and rare fish in a small tank adjacent to our desk. Boozy took a bar of soap and put it in the tank. The water started fizzing up and within a couple of weeks, small bones started appearing floating on the top of the water, and the plants flourished in reverse from brilliant green to not so radiant dead. I put Boozey's head over an active gas tap to celebrate the fish deaths, and he choked with laughter.

Hedgefund was and remains a great friend and was lucky enough to have sat next to him during English lessons too. We would always mess around throwing paper at each other, which evolved to firing stones from an elastic band at Ben Piercedears, who was another boy in our class. There was also a girl in our English lesson that was also a bit whacky and sat over the other side of the Class. I cannot remember her name because I always had a lot of things to remember. Enough was enough. We'll call her Katie Hurricane. Why not? Michael had a bit of a thing for her, and we used to write large notes on a piece of paper and hold them up to each other when the teacher turned away. They would say things such as 'you freak', or 'check out sir's eyebrow', or 'sorry I ran over your dog last Wednesday', or anything hilariously funny really.

Everybody in this lesson bizarrely enough got on formidably well with each other, barring two lads, Ben Piercedears and another lad Michael Yellhead. Ben got annoyed with Michael Yellhead on one occasion and threw a chair at him. We all laughed, then whipped out our Bacardi Breezer's and kilos of puff and got higher than ever before, but the teacher ('Monobrow' as he was more commonly known), went stark raving ballistic, and the two lads got suspended from school for a week. Science and English lessons made my last two years at school bearable and would never bunk off them. Theming the different styles of unimaginable drama, comedy, countless acts of violence, and stalking women I loved, into one lesson was the most veritable blend those sixty-five minutes needed to stick in my mind.

Time began speeding up, and GCSE season was soon amongst us. I needed to work hard and smart for these exams, or I'd end up too stupid to get a job, or even worse, become a politician. With this catastrophic amount of pressure on my shoulders, I knew that everything was going to irritate me. I wanted to start revising from as early as possible each day, so I set my alarm clock, as everyday should begin with a heart attack, opened a text book and stuck my nose in. I thought 'how is algebra going to help me later in life when it comes to mending an exhaust pipe, baking a cake, rewiring a house, or tolerating the screams of a terrified bank clerk during a heist?'. I convinced myself that maths can do one, and moved onto a bit of Geography, hoping for some pictures of a nice river or something.

An ant walked my book of flags, and I saw red mist. I necked a can of beer and leaned in a centimetre over the ant's head and performed an elongated barbaric burp until it eventually walked sideways off the page and onto the floor. I pulled out a hammer and smashed its body to pieces. It was never going to torment me again, but also, I was never going to be able to study like this. I was seething. I opted to box clever and reach out to old and new friends for a revision partner. I contacted Nicola to enrol her as assistance, but she claimed to be too busy at her own wedding. She was finally marrying Billy Lightswitch the mutant runt. Mum started banging on my bedroom door, so I scooped up all the naughty magazines off the floor and launched them under my bed. She only wanted to see how I was getting on with my revision. Bless her. I yelled through the door "unless you've got beer in your hands leave me the hell alone". She replied, "Oh are you thirsty then?". I couldn't resist but to make a plausible comment by way of response. "No, I just wanted to see if my neck leaked" I scoffed back. That one was wasted on her. Silly cow.

I narrowed down my list of potential study buddies, which resulted in Greg Fatcheese, Roxanne Beachballhead and Lisa War. I tried phoning Greg first, but his Dad said he was in an LSD induced hallucinogenic coma. I should have guessed really. I then focused my attention on Roxanne. I knew she had just returned from a holiday in Spain with her family, so I reached out to her and asked her how the holiday went. She said her Dad drizzled himself in sun tan lotion, but his genitals kept hanging out of his swimming trunks and he now has a sun burned willy and she had to look after him. I always knew they we're close, but that took the hob nobs. People would have said anything to avoid to spending time with me.

I hung up the phone, banged on the wall to tell Lola to turn the noise down on her Take That CD's, and plucked up the courage to call Lisa War. If we could study together, who knows where it might all lead. Hopefully a cheap hotel. To my amazement, Lisa said she was just about to run forty marathons backwards on her hands, tow an aeroplane up a hill in handcuffs, then after that, she would come over and revise with me in an hour. I was buzzing. I knew this was my killing ground. I scraped the crusts off my bed sheets and ran into the bathroom to shave my balls. Nobody likes a man mess down there. Mum had gone to work, and Dad was hopefully dead somewhere outside the boundaries of our house, which just left me Lola to get rid of. I bunged her a crisp £10 note to get herself some cheap alcohol to drink on the swings at the park. It worked just like every other time. I wish Mum had been responsible enough to do that for me when I was younger. Maybe I wouldn't have turned out to be such a monster. I now needed a haircut, which I couldn't do myself. My mum used to cut my hair in the 80's but she only knew two different styles, being the 'mixing bowl mullet' and when that failed, the 'Bruce Willis'.

No way was I going to Mum's place of work to ask her to stop feeding the elderly to improve my short back and sides. Every Xmas I wrote to Santa asking him to make my hair grow to the perfect all-round length then immediately stop forever, but he never delivered. My only option was to rush down to the local hair dressers, but I hate it in there. You're expected to make unnecessary small talk with the person cutting your hair and pretend to listen to them whine on about their problems. I would sit mute for five minutes then ask my hairdresser what they did for a living. They then hold a mirror up to the back of your head and stand there like a gormless rake waiting for your comments. I never know what to say when they do that. Still, needs must, I got it done. I was looking good. Really good in fact. Lisa arrived in her gym gear with a bag full of books, but I let her in anyway, and asked if she wanted a shower, to which thankfully she did. I offered to help take her clothes off, but she pushed me away and locked the door. She also mentioned something about why I had set up a discreet two-foot-long 90's camcorder on a tripod directly in front of the shower which was also recording. I attempted to explain it was just a normal thing that everybody does that these days and shut down the conversation at source. She thought I was weird for doing this and ran away screaming and crying under a towel. Yeah, like I was the weird one. I wasn't the one that brought text books to a study session. Cuckoo!!! I probably should have said that in my head and not out loud, but before my brain could compute the consequences of my words, they had already left my lips. I'd really blown it this time. Back to the drawing board.

I'd ran out of beer and felt mischievous and upset, so I decided to go into my local supermarket and approach people to tell them I was a time traveller from the year 2001 (like you do) and act all puzzled by asking them what year it is now. If they didn't runaway, scream, punch me, or cry, and answered '1998', my stock response was "which part? have France won the World Cup yet or are we still in the great zombie apocalypse of Essex?". You should have seen the blood drain from their faces. That was real entertainment. I did however have to ask other people to buy my shopping for me from thereon as I was swiftly barred from Tesco. I did meet one woman I liked, but she said she was looking for a real man. Charming! I never understood why women with fake nails, fake hair, fake eyelashes, fake boobs, fake lips, and fake tan were always looking for a real man. I prayed to God that Lisa would give me another chance and that I could find a revision partner, then BOOOM, just like Pearl Harbour, Michael Hedgefund was entering Tesco as I was being thrown out. We chatted, and he agreed to help me revise. God had answered half of my prayer. We crashed through the revision, and between us we conquered all the of the relevant subjects together. This was a meeting of the great minds and we we're going to storm the upcoming exams. I thought Hedgefund and I would probably end up going into business together and develop something where we would harvest people's most sensitive personal data without their permission, then sell it to third party companies who forever target uninterested victims with unverified spam in exchange for stupendous quantities of revenue from the advertisers. I always knew that would make a lot of money but hoped nobody else would have the audacity to think of the same scam. Sadly, somebody stole the idea from my mind years later, and I remained jealous of those happy people in TV adverts who had more fun in twenty seconds than I'd had in my entire life.

The big day had arrived, it was time to take my GCSE's. I was going to pole vault into the top grades section, make my Mum proud of me, and get a well-paid job doing something I enjoyed. I put on my 'Spliffy' jacket and set off for school. I bumped into Roxanne Beachballhead on the way to the bus stop and drew attention to my caring voice by asking how her Dad's penis was. He was on the mend still, and Roxanne appreciated the fact that I had remembered and enquired into the welfare of her Dad's private parts. I begrudgingly wished her luck with her exams and Billy Lightswitch approached me arm in arm with Nicola. It didn't phase me like it used to. I wished Nicola luck with her exams and carefully inserted a lit firework into Billy's bag when he turned his back to me. I then gritted my teeth and wished Billy the best of luck with his exams, whilst secretly hoping I got much better grades and that eventually I'd gain employment with a phenomenally senior role at the same company as him, and Billy had a significantly lower ranked and junior role, so that I could push him around and make his life a misery, then sack and bankrupt him and I'd steal Nicola from under his nose and have an expensive wedding whilst he played a second hand flute in the high street in order to avoid starvation.

As I approached my school, I felt confidently prepared for my exams, and a sense of maturity having studied with Hedgefund. I opened the main entrance door and Greg Fatcheese called out to me. I love holding doors open for people who aren't that close so I can watch them do that hopelessly silly power walk and then close it in their face as they approach, so that's exactly what I did.

When the school bell rang to denote the final exam had finished, I experienced a sense of elation. No more school. I rushed out of the assembly hall and pupils we're going potty. Greg Fatcheese had rolled a humungous drug spliff the length of the corridor and I was privileged to light it for him. He puffed and puffed whilst blasting Prodigy songs from his mini disc player. The teachers went ape, and us kids set about sporadically smashing all the fire alarms. Chaos ensued. I dressed up as Pennywise the clown and kidnapped a teacher, then dragged her by the ankles across the road into Shipwrights woods. She was not impressed. Maybe she just didn't like people who listened to Prodigy music or something else weird like that. There is no gratitude in some people.

I rushed to the petrol station to purchase my new favourite drink. Red wine. During the revision period I became hooked on the stuff. I had enough corks at home to raise the Titanic. I got unconditionally destroyed that evening, that I didn't know which planet I was on. I had a conversation with myself about how cool ears were, reflecting on the fact they could simultaneously carry headphones and sunglasses at the same time in perfect harmony. It led me to believe that ears were just like a free bag and that only a simpleton would believe their purpose was to absorb sounds and send them to the brain for processing. I was utterly away with the fairies and had to open the fridge door in the morning with sunglasses on.

CHAPTER 6 – SHAKE AND ENTER

September 1998, I had left school and I had passed all my GCSE's. My next move was to make something of my life, and I was going to cement a meaningful relation with Lisa War, or Nicola, maybe even Roxanne. I needed to go to collage or get a job, step up, help support my Mum and sister, and my other sister and my other brother who I haven't mentioned until now. There was just so much going on I didn't have time to build their characters I this book, but they were both lovely little humans and I loved them dearly. If either of you are reading this, never let it be forgotten that you both got a mention.

I purchased myself a pay as you go mobile phone the size of my arm. I could now look magnificently busy pretending to take important work calls without having a job or friends or a life. I scoured through the local papers looking at job advertisements and sourced a degree in IT at a local collage. "Bingo" I whispered to myself. I had an opportunity to get a qualification then do something associated with computers, after all, I felt the internet would have something more paramount to offer in years to come, containing more benefits than just photos of rodents in tap shoes and waistcoats or pornography. I signed up for the course there and then. Upon arrival on my first day, I was horrified to nurture that Billy Lightswitch had also signed up for the same course. I was mortified. There we're only three candidates on this course, and the other individual hid crab sticks in her socks. I was surrounded by kooks. The biggest problem with the world is that all the intelligent people were full of doubts and the stupid ones were full of confidence. God must have broken the mould when we made me, as I was both.

I couldn't face the atrocious prospect of being stuck with Billy for the next six months, so I terminated my subscription to the course and set up a temporary business, whereby for a mere £20, I would show up at a somebody's place of work in a suit and tie and beg them to take me back. I obtained a few clients under this regime, but also, I got beaten up a few times, so I secured employment as a junior at an Estate Agency in Southend to bring in some short-term Queens heads. The role had serious potential. I had access to keys of hundreds of empty properties in the Southend area and had the potential to make a lot of commission. I was tired of asking my Mum to lend me 17p every month so that I could pay it into my bank intern allowing me to withdraw £10. I had my chance, and I was going to take it. I'd always remember this opportunity, as I could hold twice as much liquid in my bladder back then than I can now. Possessing a fortuitous circuitry of internal organs is something you never forget lightly.

During my first day at the job, my new boss Marty Jobsworth tried showing me the ropes, but all I wanted to do was locate all the keys to the vacant possessions and invade Lisa. Marty was a well-educated man and joint proprietor of the business but did not stop talking. Eventually I sourced some keys and purchased some extra hyper large condoms during my lunch break. I phoned Lisa and informed her I had purchased my own business and house, and would she like to come around for a meal. She did enquire as to how at the same time the previous week I had precisely zero money, no job, and lived at home with my Mum, yet now I own my own property and business at the age of 16. I assured her that minor details weren't important, and she agreed to my proposal of dinner.

My discoloured plan had worked. All I had to was buy and fill an entire vacant house with furniture and no money then learn how to cook in two hours at work. Nothing could have been simpler. I faced an uphill battle that afternoon and concluded the day with only a blow-up bed and a takeaway menu. I pumped up the bed at the empty property, placed it in the middle of the room, and hatched a plan to obtain a free takeaway. That was the easy part, as you just get a dead animal, force it into the food, then demand it cost nothing as it renders the meal inedible. It worked every time, barring the one occasion I allegedly found an elephant in my egg fried rice. I knew I'd over reached with that one but was a pivotal learning curve. I lit a bonfire on the floor next to the bed to create the right ambience, and the scene was set. A few moments later I noticed the bed had perished to the size of a twenty pence coin and all I had now was a vacant house I was illegally trespassing in which was also in flames. This all became irrelevant as Lisa called to say she had overlooked an appointment with her dentist to discuss her broken ankle. I meandered around the flames and escaped via the back garden. As I arrived back at my Mum's, I spotted Roxanne Beachballhead returning home from walking his dog, so I reluctantly waved, only because I could see her other hand was holding a big bag of dog poo, nevertheless she did reciprocate the hand movement, thus awkwardly waggling then dropping the German shepherd's doo dah's onto the pavement, and that was the highlight of my day.

The next few days we're tense. I lost my job, faced criminal charges, and ran out of tea bags. I didn't have a clue what do, like when a good friend sits in your living room and tells you their whole family has just died and can't stop crying, and you're wondering how long you should wait before taking another bite of your cheese burger. I played drum and bass at maximum volume and mused on the cruel nature of my existence, then ventured out for a walk to clear my head. On my travels I found a discarded suitcase with £20,000 cash inside, which was nice.

I had my nose tattoo removed then returned home. Mum got up in my face and asked pointless questions such as 'what happened to your nose?', 'did you know that it's impossible to lick your own elbow?' and 'have you heard your Dad's died?'. My brain automatically switched off. I needed a night out, so I grabbed my sleeping pills and met Greg Fatcheese and Michael Hedgefund in the local pub for a non-compose mentis bender. Greg had already sunk sixty-seven pints of cider, and the pub had only been open three minutes. Michael handed me a pint of Stella and we immediately began intentionally ruining our insides with hazardous amounts of alcohol. This could have been a truly bad idea, but it takes a big person to admit when they are wrong, and an even bigger person to give a giraffe a haircut. Greg had drunk the establishment dry of alcohol then ate a bag of pure ecstasy. I had a few more pints, a bottle of tequila, and took to the microphone to perform my signature cover of the Madness' classic 'Night Boat to Cairo'. The tune was about to start, and I took a handful of sleeping pills. A nice lady approached me, and we began chatting. She told me I looked cute, and I told her that besides alcohol, there was no better feeling than putting on socks directly from the tumble dryer. She laughed considerably less than I did, then advised how it was a shame I was under six feet tall as she was looking solely for a man with my face but in excess on nine feet tall for one night of passion and eternal love. As she walked away, I placed on high heels and stood on a table then shouted, "HOW ABOUT NOW?". The pills had started to serve their purpose and I blacked out before she could reply. I awoke a week later in a place I didn't recognise. Where was I?

I felt delirious and groggy, and a nice young lady presented me with a cup of coffee. "Am I dead?" I asked the lady. She giggled. I scanned the room to check I hadn't been taken against my will, and that I had my entire body still attached to the rest of me, as you could never be too careful with my luck, however the primary signs were promising. "Hi, I'm Christie McWowwed, and this is my home" the lady said. She didn't strike me as the murderess type, but it's exactly the kind of thing that would usually happen to me, and I'd seen films before, and they all started out as normal people before brutally killing their victims in the most inhumane and unimaginable and painful ways possible. I briefly looked at her boobs before remembering they are like sun, because it was ok to look, but dangerous to stare, and that's why sunglasses were invented. I recognised her from somewhere but couldn't place it. Christie explained that I was about to perform karaoke in the pub the week before, but instead I removed all my clothes and tried to climb inside the fruit machine then collapsed on top of the Nigerian bob sleigh team. It also sounded believable, but why had I been here a week without any medical assistance or notifying somebody? I still wasn't sure if she was a serial killer or not. Christie mentioned that we we're at Secondary school together, and that was where I recognised her from. I suddenly remembered dying her hair when she fell asleep on the bus once. I looked down at my feet to see if they were in stocks next to a sledgehammer, but I was all good.

Christie was aware of my nervous persona, so to reassure me that everything was ok, she whispered in my ear "I haven't slept since that night at the pub so I could lean over your unconscious person and watch you sleep continuously for seven days straight". It didn't reassure me in the slightest. I attempted to lift myself off the sofa, but my body ached all over. "You just rest there, and I'll make you something to eat" Christie said. By now I had an alarming suspicion that she was going to kill and eat me, and just hoped it was in that order. If I was going to die, I wanted to go out with a blaze of glory, maybe by kicking an already angry bear in the shin or be launched out of a roller coaster at its fastest and most unsafe point. Nobody wants to die on a sofa. Christie returned with a bowl of tomato soup and the best cup of tea I'd ever consumed, so I moved in with her and we entered in to a serious relationship before I finished the last sip. This was only the beginning for my alter ego better known as 'Curseanova'!

Christie helped me secure a good job in London, I passed my driving test, and after a year of living together, I decided to purchase some aquatic fish. Greg Fatcheese bet me three thousand pounds that I wouldn't place a bunch of wasps up inside my bottom and let them build a nest. It was the easiest money I ever made. I mean, I couldn't sit down for months afterwards but I had enough money to purchase a tank full of expensive water wizards. I heated the tank to correct temperature and released the fish from their bags into the tank. It looked magical and was worth every sting.

I stepped away from the tank to admire its beauty, and Christie came bursting though the door with a face like thunder. "YOU'VE LEFT SKID MARKS IN THAT BLOODY TOILET AGAIN!", she yelled at the top of her lungs.

For a young man that had a comment to make about everything I was left speechless. She had been warning me about this for months, and I had promised to be more considerate in the bathroom as she had already threatened to leave me over it. I placed my head into my hands and looked up to find Christie had scooped all the fish out of my tank and into a bucket, then ran into the bathroom and locked the door behind her. I repeatedly hammered on the door begging for an opportunity to rectify the situation, but it was too late. She had flushed all my expensive fish down the toilet, unlocked the door, and nudged past me saying nothing. I peered over the toilet to find my favourite shark fish (Albert the sex pest) flapping around on the surface of the water. Without a moment's hesitation, I stuck my arm down the toilet and air lifted him out, but it was too late. Albert was dead. A life for a wipe. I tried giving him mouth to mouth to no avail. All my friends we're now dead and making their way out to sea, whilst I was left with an angry girlfriend and skid marks on my fist. Christie told me I had to sleep on the sofa that night. On a good day, it generally took me about fifteen hours to get to sleep of an evening, however I cried all through the night on this occasion. In the morning I spent hours making Christie butter on toast by way of an apology breakfast, opened the bedroom door, and found a severely ugly boy reassembling a rodent making sympathy love to her.

I dropped the plastic plate of toast in shock and Christie told me to give her a few hours then come back. I went into the living room as ordered, then unreservedly minding my own business, placed a glass to the wall and secretly listened to Christie and the rodent have inadequate intercourse for approximately two hours and twelve minutes. I was petrified of being single but knew Christie and I had reached the end of the road. No girlfriend of mine flushed my fish down the toilet, slept with somebody else, and then to add insult to injury, refused to eat carefully crafted toast I had lovingly made her without getting away with it. I was almost certain I'd leave her to do the washing up as a form of seriously evil reprisal, and that would teach her to cheat on me, so I did. I grabbed a bag of my things and left. I returned five minutes later to do the washing up and run the hoover round but then I left again properly. It never ceased to amaze me how bending down to pick up a tiny crisp crumb would take one second, yet I'd still rather stand up and run over it three thousand times with the hoover for a week at different angles until I'd won.

On my first evening as a single and homeless young man, I found it a lot to fathom. I took a deep breath and stock of my options, then narrowed it down to four possible actions. My first idea was to ask Christie to stop cheating on me and take me back, but I wasn't prepared to do the washing up again. Mt second master plan was to visit my Mum and ask her if I could have my old room for the evening, then host a micro rave around my bed to make loads of money then move out. The third option was to contact Lisa War and tell her I'd been swallowed by a whale but ran ever so quickly down its body and found my way to day light again. I had used this attention seeking dilemma before, and she didn't buy it then, so I'd be surprised if this feeble recycled story would have her rush to my aid. The final option was to break into a toy shop and steal all their Lego, then make a house out of it in the woods. I'd convinced myself this was the best thing I'd ever contemplated doing, and if it wasn't for the urgency, I would have fulfilled this fantasy, but it was snowing, so I made an imaginary sleeping bag and set up camp in a bus stop.

As I was on the cusp of falling asleep and freezing towards a guaranteed death, a mammoth lorry pulled into the bus lane, and fly tipped three thousand bags of Lego. I couldn't believe it. The driver then abandoned the lorry with a full tank of petrol and left the keys in the ignition. I pondered for a while, and assessed what kind of Lego bricks they were, and to my horror, I learned there were more yellow pieces than blue. Dissatisfied with the colour of the bricks and the gift horse that fell into my lap, I decided to hop into the lorry anyway, and drove into the woods to renovate my new house. I put together a modest home, and within seconds of clicking the last brick into place, a bat signal from an unknown source lit up the sky, alerting every single drug addict, murderer, rapist, wolf, and pneumatic drill wielding possessed violent criminal within a twelve County radius to my exact GPS coordinates. It was too cold to fight them all off, so I retired for the evening, safely inside my bomb proof Lego house, and listened to the blissful howling and torturous screams.

I'd never been this cold before. It reminded me of when I was at school, as we had an outdoor swimming pool. In winter, our PE teacher would hire a JCB to smash through the first metre of ice on the surface of the pool before the lesson, then allow us to dive through the hole. You either swam until you were purple or died in those lessons. Great memories. The Lego house was a complete waste of time, like all the carrier bags people hoard under their sinks and never use again, only with less disturbances and hyperthermia. I should have gone to my Mum's house as she would have looked after me, as blood was thicker than water. Then again gravy was thicker than blood, so maybe a roast dinner should have been the most important thing in my life!

I gathered together the loose change in my pockets, deserted the Lego house and made my way hastily to the off license for a crate of cold lagers to warm me up. Whenever I found money in my pocket that I didn't know I had, I always thought that God was rewarding me for being sexy. I needed to very promptly befriend a stranger and con them into helping me. I spotted a gentleman in front of me in the queue holding a basket that contained a bottle of economy vodka, paracetamol, a tube of reduced Pringles, a book of crosswords, and copy of Jumanji on DVD.

I suggestively placed my now tattoo free nose into his collection of items, then looked up at him square in the eyes and said, "you must be single", to which he replied, "how did you know?". "Because you are pig ugly' I crowed. He didn't strike me as the pen pal type and rammed a bag of Wotsits up my nose. Making new friends was hard. I placed my cans on the counter, paid for the drinks, and the cashier asked me if I'd like a receipt. I remember this episode well, as I checked my pockets, and realised I had nothing in them, so it would have been nice to have a small piece of paper to screw up and throw on the floor as I left the shop, so I replied "DEFINITLY". As I left the store, a nice lady smiled at me, so I utilised my signature move by intrusively shaking one of the cans up and down and opened it against my chest to ensure the entire volume sprayed over my top and face, because I liked to mess up relationships before they happened.

CHAPTER 7 – TURD GIRL

I sat on the swing at my local park and put my brain to work on thinking about how I could turn my life around whilst knocking back industrial strength lager. I used to be so cool. Once I ripped a phone book in half, and all the bridesmaids at my Uncle's wedding turned around because they were captivated by my performance and hardness, and now I was projectile vomiting on a strip of tarmac. I had always imagined that by this point in my life I would have had a high-flying well-paid career, own a fleet of super yachts, and have impeccable dress sense. Instead I was riddled with debt, had zero boats, and wore Xmas socks in June.

I trampled another empty can of lager and thrust it against the outer fence from distance, when I noticed the dog poop bin wobbling erratically out the corner of my eye. I staggered over to investigate, and I was surprised by the outcome of my findings. Upon lifting the lid on the dog poop bin and peering inside, a woman was staring back at me. A very beautiful woman. "What are you doing inside a dog poo bin?" I asked her. "The last thing I remember is being in a club and allowing totally unknown men to buy me endless glasses of white wine with visible purple fizzing lumps present" she spoke back. I stuck my arm between some little dirty bags and pulled the woman out of the bin. She smelled divine. "Thank you" she said, "My name is Kathy Heavens". Kathy went on to question me as to why I was alone in a park at midnight going through dog poop bins as I wiped the excrement off her face. I offered Kathy the last swig of backwash in my final can, and we chatted until day light on the see saw. It transpired she had a grand career, was humorous, highly intelligent, had a high energy, and was beautiful under her recent face paint, but was clumsy when it came to the intake of alcohol and resurfacing in unusual places.

We exchanged a private joke that if we ever got together and friends and family asked how we met, we'd simply respond 'work'. We both fractured our necks laughing at that one. With it becoming apparent she wasn't an utter bum, I knew I'd have to go the extra mile to impress her if I wanted to formulate a stronger connection with her, so I head butted a flower bed, and told her I was building my own property surrounded by nature. Kathy was fascinated and insisted she viewed it there and then. As we entered the woods, weaved in an out of all the syringes, and came face to face with my Lego house, Kathy's premonition of built in wardrobes with a shoe corridor leading to an ensuite bathroom flat out evaporated. "As I said, there is still a long way to go, and a roof should be going on soon" I said. It was only then that Kathy revealed she had her own flat with its own roof, and I felt like one of those recklessly thick people that couldn't reach the £1,000 mark on 'Who wants to be a millionaire'. It wasn't game over just yet, as Kathy and I had bonded at the park and she agreed to let me take her out for a meal. Kathy said she was a virgin, then phoned one of her boyfriends to pick her up from the woods, which I did not find strange one iota, and I moved back home to my Mum's house to plan my date. My Mum didn't live at the property anymore, as I detected when I entered the vacant house and found a twenty pence coin taped to a floor board with a note that read 'hi son, I've emigrated, get yourself a Curly Wurly'. I'd never felt more loved.

A few days later, Kathy and I had our big first date. Kathy worked around the corner from the offices where I worked, so I asked her where she would like to go with a simple coin toss, whereby if the penny came down, we would go wherever she chose, and if it stayed suspended in the air forever, I got to pick. Kathy opted for a venue within walking distance of our work locations, and I suggested our lunch break as opposed to an evening, as it would be easier for her to runaway within an hour and remove my existence from her mind, rather than drag out an uncomfortable evening of dull suffering and heavy drinking then wind up in sewage plant waiting for another good Samaritan to rescue her. She agreed. As the time grew closer to lunch, I began to get the sweats, and sheer panic rushed through my veins.

I'd never been on a date with a stunning faithful woman that may or may not arrive with one of her boyfriends. I was also greedy when it came to food and became fearful of my two stomachs. If I couldn't finish my lunch because my normal belly was completely full, I feared my back up snack belly would devour a large bag of Haribo bears and a multipack of salt n vinegar crisps, and I would look like a corpulent pig. This would have been a disaster. I went into the works loo and emptied my bowels as best I could, then took a slow walk to the agreed meeting point. As I approached, I saw Kathy swigging liquid from a secret compartment sewn into her skirt, and I helped her off the floor. "Hello beautiful" I said. I way trying hard not to appear too keen. "Who are you?" she replied. I refreshed her memory, and the waiter escorted us to our table. I ordered the classic burger with chips and a half pint of Shandy. Kathy ordered a bread roll and a Jeroboam of neat Absinthe. The conversation flowed smoothly, and Kathy told me she liked me. She had obviously run out of things to say just lied to pass the time, but I powered down my brain and believed her forthwith. I let her into a secret by telling her how I keep a notepad next to my bed, so that if I woke up in the night with a brilliant idea, I could write it down. She was enthralled by everything I had dreamed about, including the one where I scribbled down about strobe light hats for owls, only I wasn't entirely sure what I meant by it, however I was quietly confident I was on the cusp of something walloping. The date was going well.

Kathy left the table to go to the toilet half way into our lunch date and forgot where she was upon her return to reunite with me to continue our lunch. She sat down at a table full of men all telling each other hyper sexist jokes, and so she joined in with them and handed out business cards. It was right there and then that I knew she was 'the one'. I went over to her new table and removed her tongue from one of the men's mouths. "Apologies gentlemen, this hot pocket rocket is with me" I worryingly recited. They picked up ash trays and broke them on my skull. Thankfully Kathy began sobering up, and she left the yuppies to their over exaggerated storytelling. I placed a pile of napkins over my head to slow the bleeding and followed her out. Kathy realised she had left her lipstick and knickers in the toilet, so we had to go back. I was scared than the time I had a nightmare about a clown using a ventriloquist dummy. The boisterous table of so-called men all stood up and walked towards us, hence we both retreated hastily having pulled Kathy back from, advancing towards them waggling her knickers. I carried Kathy back to work, gave her a kiss on the cheek, and she went in for the kill. I couldn't resist a quick snog, as despite her flaws, something kept drawing me towards her. Kathy then collapsed in the reception area of her building, so I left her there to nap as I needed to return to work. This was a triumph for me, as I'd never been on a first date where the lady didn't sleep with someone else or stab me with a steak knife. Kathy was special. Upon arrival at my office, I got stuck in the revolving door with a woman from another team, so I counted it as a date.

Over the coming weeks and months, Kathy and I started to get serious with each other, and despite a few dubious events I put down to my paranoia concerning her seeing other people, we we're genuinely happy together. Kathy even went one of those days without consuming a bottle of white wine, so she treated herself to a wheelbarrow full to the brim with neat Russian vodka to celebrate. She started going for runs along the seafront to help keep her clean of drink, and she'd return every night saying, "my legs ache", "I'm getting fitter", and "I need to phone Michael and see if I left my knickers round there earlier". I felt that now was the right time to invite myself to live with her, as we could be blissfully happy together, and make it water tight impossible for her to cheat on me. We snuggled up on the sofa to watch a romantic film together, and I began planning the speech in my head. As I pressed play on the 'Human Centipede', the DVD started with a warning advising "this film contains adult scenes", to which I turned to

Kathy and said "yet I never actually see anybody putting the washing machine on, doing a food shop, going to work, or paying their council tax, so why do they lie?". Kathy dropped to the floor and rolled around deep belly laughing for hours then forcefully pinned me to the carpet and sexually attacked me. It was quintessential. I rushed round to my Mum's house, and asked Lola to help me pack up my things, then placed Kathy into a hypnotic spell using excessive amounts alcohol to coerce her into believing that me moving in with her was a first class and legendary idea. My hoodwinking had worked, so I unpacked my only pair of pants, extensive collection of drum n bass vinyl's, and my empty fish tank in her abode.

With my relationship going cosily with Kathy, I was eventually introduced to her family. They we're truly a pleasant band of people. Kathy's sister Josie was a down to Earth straight shooter and was a breath of fresh air to be around. Josie lived with her husband who was a human shaped ball of hair. Nothing more needs to be said about that. I then met her Mum and her other half who sold pegs seven days a week, and her nameless gay brother. Then the time came for the person she was dreading me meeting most. Her Dad. To be fair, I wasn't looking forward to it either, not because he was bad in any way, but we all know how over protective Dad's can be of their daughters, and I was brimming with nerves. It perturbed me that her Dad might not be over zealous about his daughter dating a twenty-two-year-old with the bank balance of a toddler. My credit score was simply a picture of a monkey playing a tambourine. Deep down I was a good person, but I never carried a shovel around with me to prove it. On the day of meeting her dad, Kathy discovered that her gym bag held six bottles of wine and a bendy straw, so she threw it over her shoulders, and headed out the door to spend the day drinking with Josie. I spent the day mentally preparing myself for the evening meet with her Dad, which was also a house warming party, therefore remained sober, and kept myself occupied. I pretended to be an American rapper in the 90's by performing sign language in the mirror whilst lowering my jeans to my ankles so far that I began dragging them eight feet behind me on a bit of rope. Like you do. Once in the zone, and headstrong, I set off to meet Kathy and Josie, before heading to their dad's house.

As I strolled down the street with my headphones on to meet Kathy and Josie, I put some loose change into a homeless man's cup, only to find it was a normal guy just enjoying his coffee whilst waiting for a bus, so that was exclusively awkward. I prayed I would never looked like him. I also prayed for a job where I only worked one hour a week and got paid a million pounds a minute. I stopped in a shop for chewing gum and farted during the loudest part of a song so that nobody would notice, then remembered I was wearing headphones. The shop emptied and I looked down at my jeans to confirm that I had followed through. I sprinted home to change my jeans and called Kathy on the way to let her know I was running late due to an un fart related incident. Josie answered the phone because Kathy was otherwise engaged fighting a lamp post. I became overwhelmed with bad thoughts about the evening ahead. Kathy was going to be obliterated in front of an important audience upon which I knew nobody. Thankfully the human shaped ball of hair was driving, so I would know somebody else sober I had met before, and he kindly agreed to pick me up on the way to scoop up Kathy and Josie from the public house. On the way we drove past a huge boy sitting on a seesaw by himself, so we pulled over to see if another child fell out of the sky. We waited patiently for half an hour, but it didn't happen, and we left disappointed. As we arrived at the pub, we witnessed Kathy climbing out of a dog poop bin. I thought to myself 'here we go again'. Josie had the look of actual death plastered across her face as even she was embarrassed. After a loud drive, we all arrived at Kathy and Josie's dad's house. There we're balloons on the door and many people entering the property. This was it. My heart was pounding inside my body like a brick in a knackered old washing machine on quick spin. Kathy and Josie weaved towards their Dad who was waiting on the door step with open arms for them and began cuddling whilst the human shaped ball of hair and I pigeon stepped fifty metres behind them.

Kathy's dad caught my eye, stuck his arm out in front of me, and shook my hand. "You must be Jamie" he said. The man was smiling, so maybe he didn't want to gut me from forehead to big toe as I had fully anticipated, but still lent on an heir of caution in case it was a trap to lull me in under a false sense of security and yank my shoulder clean out of the socket then weld me to an active train track. "Very nice to meet you" I replied whilst pulling my quivering hand away. Kathy's dad invited me in and told me to make myself at home, nevertheless I refrained from getting naked and drinking a bottle of whiskey on the sofa. I was offered an alcoholic drink but opted for a can of coke as I had to remain in control for Kathy's sake, besides it was fun to trick my liver occasionally. We we're a team now, and there is no 'I' in team. There are however six I's in 'Kathy is drinking white wine out of a cuckoo clock again'.

Kathy was a mess, and I was stone cold sober in front of fifty people I didn't know. Josie and her nameless gay brother came and stood with me whilst Kathy struggled to nail the Dad's clock back to the wall. "How are you feeling ducky boy?" her brother asked me, then rubbed my thigh with his groin. I was never going to make it through the evening sober, so I went into the kitchen to fix myself a cocktail. With Kathy and Josie being well oiled, I tackled playing catch up, and poured myself a pint of vodka. I drank three pints in thirty seconds, when unanticipatedly my alimentary canal went into spasm. Half of Europe fell out of my mouth and onto Kathy's Dad's brand-new carpet. Everybody was looking at me in disgust. My internal organs were all over the floor. Thankfully there was no social media in those days, or I would have been an overnight sensation and retired on the royalties from the platform it was uploaded to. Kathy was livid and made a point of telling me so, but oddly enough, her Dad helped me up and assisted me wiping a lung off my face. That was the last thing I remember of that evening. It is alleged that I passed out and was carried into the spare bedroom, to which I awoke a few hours later and almost punched a taxi driver because I wanted to get home and they wouldn't accept me on account of my drunken attitude. I could truly believe this sequence of events took place, but my fundamental concern was facing the music, as I had lavishly messed up, and for all the many things Kathy had done wrong in our relationship, the limelight was now firmly on me, and I had some bottoms to kiss if I didn't want to be on the scrap heap again.

I awoke the next morning with a mouth so dry and smelly it felt like somebody had held my mouth wide agape and allowed twelve baboons to empty their load between my teeth. I didn't know where I was, I could barely open my eyes, and I felt like my head had been runover by a steamroller. It slowly became apparent that I was on my Mum's sofa yet had no recollection of how I got there, as I didn't know where she lived. I noticed my coat on the floor, but there was no sign of Kathy or anybody else for that matter. I called Kathy and she was dejectedly cross with me. I held the phone some distance from my ear for an hour or so, whilst she screamed out the events of the previous night. I was mortified to hear that I'd left a shot of vodka in one of the bottles. I begged her to meet me for a pizza, and after a lot of gentle persuasion, she finally agreed. I jumped into my Mum's shower, then straight back out again as I still had my clothes on. Not something I said often. As I arrived half dead to the pizza place, a hot waitress kept flirting with me. She was all "table for one again?" and "are you ready to order the usual?". I was batting straight back with idiosyncratic pick up lines such as "what font is this menu in?" and "I might have lasagne, but I might not", so I was pretty much playing hard to get, as I was desperate to make things up with Kathy. She was already half an hour late, so I continued watching all the hardcore cyclists pushing their bodies to the limit and roaring past the window. It almost gave me the motivation to stand up and wipe the cheese off my T shirt.

After an hour I had received the message loud and clear that Kathy wasn't interested in my many apologies, and I left the restaurant sadder than I'd ever been. I got into my car and decided to go for a drive to clear my head. I was stopped by the Police and the Officer in question asked me if I knew why I had been pulled over. I said it was probably because it was too windy to chat on the motorway at 103mph, to which the Officer did not find amusing. I had to blow into a breathalyser, and I was stunned by the result. I had chicken pox. No, in all seriousness, I had blown over the legal alcohol limit to drive. My car was seized, and I lost my driving license for a year. I didn't need it anyway, as if there was one thing I had recently remembered about the night before, it's that no matter how many times you try, cash points won't give you money if you put your driving license in by mistake. That's seven hours of my life I'd never get back.

As I began my 35 mile walk home, I received a phone call from Kathy. I couldn't believe it. She had been reflecting on all the bad things she had done and concluded that I shouldn't be punished for one mistake. She even agreed to come and pick me up. I'm not just saying this, but I had never been happier than at this moment in time, except for the day my boss was off sick, and I made a matching paperclip bracelet and necklace combo. I saw Kathy arriving in the distance when she stopped and waited for me to walk alongside a deep puddle so that she could whizz past and drown me. I clambered inside the passenger side of her car and repeatedly apologised for getting so drunk and promised it would never happen again. We kissed and made up. We went home and Kathy headed straight to the wine rack and poured a vase of white, but I daren't have muttered a word about it as I was still rigidly in the dog house.

I was still in a state of elation that the women I genuinely wanted to spend the rest of my life had agreed to give us another go. She spent the evening getting wasted, and accidentally ate three tennis balls, because let's face it, Pringles really need a new packaging manager to cater for drunk people. I sat on the naughty chair going through my spam emails wondering how lucky I was to have Kathy, and what the odds must have been for me to win the Nigerian lottery so many times. If I'd have taken up all the Viagra offers sent to me, I'd have been able to run a three-legged race by myself.

For the next few years, I was a squeaky-clean boyfriend and never once put a foot out of place, whilst Kathy got drunk blind five days a week, and often missed her last train home, leaving her stranded in London at 2am. Kathy would often burst into the bedroom during the early hours of the morning whilst I was asleep, and shout "DO YOU THINK I'M DRUNK?", and I'd wake up frozen with hysteria learning how it felt to be an untrained bomb disposal expert wondering whether to cut the green or the pink wire to save humanity. As luck would have it, bad luck mainly, I had my driving license reinstated, and was able to collect her every time going forward. I was aware that I had become the fourth emergency service for her, but there was nothing else I would rather be doing at 2am than getting woken up to drive thirty miles to locate my comprehensively drunk girlfriend flirting with potential rapists outside bars. I was the lucky one and had to remember that.

I was never sure how many cartwheels was 'too many', whenever I approached her to let her know her carriage awaited. In hindsight I should have attempted to initiate a new form of sign language to her from across the bar, but last time I did that I ended up being in eight gangs. On one occasion I had been redecorating Kathy's second bedroom when I received a notification earlier than usual to inform me that she was drunk. It was only 10pm and well ahead of schedule. She called to say she had missed her last train. The last train didn't leave until after midnight, and she was making precisely zero sense. This wasn't the normal drunk Kathy I knew, and something was almost definitely wrong. Worried about her, I put down the brushes, and covered to from head to toes in paint, I drove into London to check she was ok. Upon arrival I was declined entry to the bar Kathy was allegedly in, as it was a smartly dressed bar in the City of London. I had magnolia paint all down my clothes and face and was trying to gain access to a prestigious wine bar. The security guards must have thought I'd breached the perimeter of my padded cell and headed straight there. I pleaded with them to allow me a moment's entry to check Kathy was ok as she was not answering her phone, but to no avail. I waited in the car like a good little dog and continued to call her for another hour. My irritation level was above maximum. Whenever I got this angry, I'd close my eyes and convince myself things could be worse, by imagining I am a tree that spent decades growing only to be cut down and made into a Boyzone scrapbook. This didn't work today as I was too wound up and the journeys were costing me hundreds of pounds per month in petrol. Being alive was so expensive!

Eventually I spotted Kathy floundering out of the wine bar, hand in hand with her work colleague Chris. I had met this slippery imbecilic waste of skin once before, and I didn't like him then. He tried to kiss her, and my blood turned to molten lava. I surged out of the car and ran towards them. Chris saw me coming and ran away in the opposite direction and Kathy was all over the place. She couldn't speak, she didn't know where she was, and couldn't stand up. I'd seen her drunk so many times to realise that this was much more than a regular drunken episode. Kathy's drink had been spiked by Chris, and if I hadn't have showed up when I did, I dread to think what would have happened to her. Chris was not only a hideous degenerate, but also uncommonly tight fisted and made Kathy pay for all his drinks. Chris had his own girlfriend but refused to take her to the cinema because he would rather wait seventeen years to watch a film for free on TV. He was also cocky and thought he was good looking because he went on tanning beds, although his appearance was less 'sun kissed' and more 'Dorito assaulted'. He was the mirror opposite of good looking and I passionately hated single element of him. I would go as far to say that I hated Chris more so than Billy Lightswitch. I ladled Kathy up, fireman carried her to my car, and slumped her into the passenger seat. I stopped to get he some water from a petrol station, but Kathy refused to drink it, and I deliberated taking her to hospital. Under duress, I eventually managed to force some water down Kathy's throat, and she nonchalantly came back to life. It was a good sign when she remembered who I was and heaved up a few yards of vegetable soup over my legs and doors. I was swimming in the stuff.

I stopped the engine to remove some of the substance that prevented me seeing over the steering wheel, and then the car would not start, and we we're still a good ten miles from home. I lifted the car bonnet and switched on the torch. I was terrible when it came to mechanics, but then I noticed a dead spider lying of the oil cap. I thought I must have needed a new spider, so I began wading through the grass at the side of the road trying to find an alive one so that we could be on our way. Unbeknown to me, Kathy was a dab hand with cars, and when I returned to the vehicle, she had taken the gearbox apart and mended it. God knows where she found a spider from in the dark in her state, but well played to her.

Once back at home, I tucked Kathy into bed, made her a cup of tea, and asked her is she remembered kissing Chris. She shot up out of bed and went crackers. For such a small lady she could knock you off your feet with the wind of her voice. "I NEVER F*CKING KISSED HIM" she bellowed into the next post code. Clearly my own eyes had been telling my brain fibs, and the noise was too much to handle. I waited for her to pass out again, tucked her into bed, set her alarm, and went to my Mum's to stay for the night, now I knew where she lived. Kathy had lots of text messages from different men offering some quite sexually explicit content, and I noticed one from the ugly cretin Chris reading simply 'sorry, maybe next time'. I was going to make him pay for what he'd done to Kathy. He had the word 'twat' written right through him like a stick of Seaside rock, but he was going to meet a timely demise having drugged and attempted to take advantage of my girlfriend.

The next day I received a call from Kathy asking where I was. I filled her in on what had happened, and she claimed not to remember any of it. She even lied to me by stating that she got a taxi home which cost £108, which was a very precise figure for a sinister fabrication of the truth. We all bend the truth from time to time, like when I took a married friend's phone, and changed my name to 'Chloe from the sex brothel', then repeatedly called him at 3am, but this was a deliberate sabotage of the acts that took place. I agreed to meet Kathy for lunch, and she was full of remorse, balling her eyes out, and vowed never to be so unaware of her surroundings ever again. Kathy then asked the Waitress for a bottle of wine and she asked Kathy how many glasses she would like. Kathy replied, "it's already in a glass so I'll just take a straw with that", and ripped the bottle clean out of the Waitresses hand. We hugged it out and that evening set up a Ouija Board to summon the actual devil then played Sonic the Hedgehog. A day later I located Chris and launched a full tin of magnolia paint directly into his eyes that was left over from the decorating, and cable tied his arms and legs together. I put him in the boot of my car and drove him to Switzerland, upon which I shaved his penis off with a cheese grater. My girlfriend would be the last person he tried putting his lop-sided maggot where it wasn't wanted. I screamed 'MUG' in his ear and threw his balls at him.

Life slowly returned to normality, with Kathy and I were in a good place since she had cut down on her drinking. We were both doing well in our jobs, and we enjoyed weekends with Kathy's sister Josie and the human shaped ball of hair, and occasionally I acted out the worm dance by choice. Kathy had even cut down on the late nights of getting wasted with men she thought were just friends who were desperately forcing themselves upon her. We'd go for meals together, play ten pin bowling, and be super geeks on quiz machines at our local snooker hall. Kathy was showing more interest in me by upping the number of text messages she would send me per day from none to fourteen hundred. When a lady texts you that many times a day, she either likes you, or wants to kill you, so I had my fingers crossed that she liked me a bit. On one occasion, Kathy and I went to Spain together and bought drugs from a man being chased by Police for selling fake sunglasses. My financial situation had significantly improved to a point a cash point shot out a burst of confetti to congratulate me on having enough funds to pull out a £10 note with only twenty-seven days until payday. Life was magical at that moment, but then the dominos began to fall. I was singled out and called into a meeting at work with HR, and the only reason HR ever called somebody into their department was to break bad news. On the morning of the meeting I held up four ties and asked Kathy which one she thought looked best on me for my meeting, and she said they were all nice. Later in the day she asked me how my meeting went, and I said I looked ridiculous wearing all four ties. We laughed and laughed, and I then I told her I'd been sacked, but still we laughed and laughed some more and then I cried.

A poisonous weasel on my team at work called Saul Hater was jealous that I was vastly more intelligent than him, and I was doing a far greater job the he could ever dream of, so he had invented a technical crime that never happened involving fraud, and HR instantly believed him without researching the matter and asked me to leave. Saul was a pedantic snake from day 1 and had the appearance of a semi deflated bouncy castle. Saul had been trying to push me out of the company for some time, only I had to tread carefully with my revenge as he was partially brain damaged and would often use his mental illness as an excuse to get away whatever he so desired. I had no job or money coming in, and Kathy didn't like it, which was fair enough, as I wasn't delirious about the situation myself. It caused endless arguments between us, but I did attempt to take my case to a Judge, when the company lost their bottle and my settled loss of wages out of Court, as they knew they didn't have a legal leg to stand on. The fact remained that I still had no job, and I had a gut feeling that my next communication with Kathy would begin with her dumping me and finish with "I'd like it if we could stay friends," which translates from Female to English as "I want to have sex with people who are aren't you".

A month passed and I was still unable to find another job. I spent all day searching intensely whilst blowing my out of court settlement on internet bingo. I was prepared to take a pay cut and even try something new, but the employment options were simply not there. Kathy slipped back to her old ways and began heavily drinking daily with unknown men again. She would brush her teeth before breakfast then moan her wine tasted funny. I'd have friends notify me that they had spotted Kathy out looking very cosy with other guys. It was destroying me. One day I slid out of bed at midday and immediately walked to the shop to purchase something to soothe the crippling anxiety. Typically, this was the one day I saw Roxanne Beachballhead for the first time in over a decade, and she was glammed up in expensive designer clothes and getting out of her husband's Ferrari when she spotted me. I was unwashed in Spiderman pyjamas clutching twelve cans of cider and a toilet brush. She asked me if I wanted any professional help, but I couldn't understand why. After trawling job sites for almost six weeks, I finally got an interview. The location was nowhere near where I wanted to be, and meant I would be miles away from Kathy, but I had to secure the position and start bringing in some money again. This made Kathy happy knowing that I would have money for us and that she would see me less. On the day, I signed in at the reception area, and the lady interviewing me came to meet me. She went to give me a handshake, but I'd already started leaning in for an open mouth kiss, and somehow, I didn't think that was a good start.

I hadn't had an interview for many years, so I was a little rusty, nevertheless, I sat down and attempted to answer every question fired at me. I had to get this job there and then, as one of Kathy's friends was getting married in Turkey in a few months' time, and I had to go, but needed the funds to make it possible. I performed better than I expected under pressure, which may have led to a hint of complacency when the interviewer asked me if I had any questions for her. I paused for a moment and replied, "do you think Tom Hanks signs his Christmas cards 'T Hanks' to save time by rolling his name and a nice message into one?". The interviewer and her two colleagues sat in complete silence for a few seconds, then ushered me to the door. The lady said that on a scale of highly unlikely to impossible, I would not get the job after such a car crash interview, but as I was cute (her words not mine), and made her uncontrollably laugh in deafening straight faced silence with the Tom Hanks question, she would try and pull a few strings to get me on the payroll. I will forever be in debt to that lady, as low and behold, I got the job. Well done me. In a joint effort, Kathy and I made a celebratory meal together that evening, which meant I spent hours cooking all the food from scratch whilst she drank wine and watched me across the work surface hiccupping. Things were looking up again. We could go to Turkey and enjoy a well earned break away together for her friend's wedding. I would also have the money to get Kathy a better present for her impending birthday this year, as she despised it when I bought her a joint Christmas and Birthday present, but that's what she gets for being born in June. I loved sleep and I slept like a log that night. For me, sleep was scintillating, because you weren't dead, but you weren't awake either, so it was a win-win situation. Waking up EVERY day was a bit excessive though.

On the first day of my new job I was running late, so to save time getting ready, I ate my cereal in the shower, which oddly added another forty-five minutes to my preparation. I knuckled down at my new job and worked with a great team of people. I was so much happier at this firm in comparison to my old company where I work with a bunch of egotistical morons. My band of colleagues here were receptive and honourable people. I felt that this new job was what Kathy and I needed to progress with our future. My goal was to save up the money for Turkey, have an awesome time there, and then stash some earnings into a savings account for an engagement ring to propose to Kathy with. Turkey was now only a month away, and whilst I was excited, Kathy kept going missing most evenings and developing a rare form of amnesia whereby she was genetically incapable of answering here mobile phone or sending text messages. Apparently, there is no medical term for this type of deficient brain activity, so I just believed what Kathy told me and ordered myself not to research anything further into it. I was now frequently finishing work and returning home to spend evenings alone. I'd be sitting in front of the TV whilst tightly gripping my phone in my hand and waiting for a call from Kathy to request a lift home any of the usual locations, which ranged from various London establishments to a man's house twenty miles away in Billericay. I was perturbed and frightened for her, as she trusted the wrong people after a few drinks, and I'd call and call and call her, but she would respond with a cryptic text messages that said, "STOP calling me". What's that supposed to mean? I had to phone her another eighty-seven times to find out what she meant.

I needed the Turkey holiday to happen a lot sooner than it was scheduled for as it had become painfully obvious that Kathy had fallen out of love with me and was entering a period of distance prior to an inevitable break up. She no longer realised how handsome my nan said I was. A week before we we're due to fly to Turkey, Kathy discovered that two of the thirty people flying out to the wedding were ex conquests of hers. Kathy plucked up the

courage to tell me, and I was not dazzled by the thought of it, and she became increasingly edgy about it, as if she hadn't quite given me all the information I should have been furnished with. Within the next few days of take-off, Kathy went missing for longer periods of time than usual, and then the day before we we're due to leave for the wedding, she dumped me without any explanation via a text message. It was officially over between us. The dream had ended. Gallons of liquid left my eyes for hours. I'd never been savagely heartbroken before. The highlight of that evening for me was when I whispered "I believe in second chances" to the last Haribo bear I picked up off the floor, then bit it's head off like a wild dog destroying a squeaky toy. It was too late to have my flights and accommodation refunded, and the couple getting married from not from my group of friends. Kathy returned home legless to find me asleep on the sofa. She woke me up and we had a half sensible discussion. We agreed that we would both go to Turkey together, but only as friends, whilst pretending to be together given the short notice, then tell everyone we'd split up upon our return to England.

I was so cut up by the situation that I stupidly agreed to the farcical offered. The only reason I grabbed it with both hands, was because sub consciously I was hoping that we would get out there and maybe patch things up. It was a long shot, but I loved her too much to not trial it. This was my last chance to pull out all the stops and I had two weeks to win her heart, otherwise I had lost her forever. The pressure was on. I went for a drive and stopped to get Kathy and I some dinner from the drive thru, only to discover my driver side window had broken and no longer opened. I worried I'd starve to death. In the end I managed to get the food, and rushed home for an unromantic and sexless evening with the women I loved.

CHAPTER 8 – THE DALAMAN SEX MONSTER

The big day had finally arrived. Kathy and I we're off to Turkey for her friend's wedding, to which we we're attending as friends whilst pretending to be a couple until she officially dumps me in two weeks. I pledged that this wasn't going to happen as I was going to woo her in front of two other men she had previously slept with and secretly still liked.

Absolutely nothing could go wrong. We travelled two hours to the airport together in complete silence, starting the day at boss level. I sat outside the duty-free section licking a lollipop for breakfast, and Kathy sat quarter of a mile away from me pretending she wasn't aware of my existence until her friends arrived. I was informed by a tourist that if you're an adult eating a lollipop, you're either a sexy lady or the creepiest man at Stansted. There was no middle ground apparently. What a berk. Kathy's friends all arrived, and she set a two-week timer on her phone labelled 'Freedom Day' then re-introduced me to her life. I met the couple that were getting married in a few days' time, and thankfully they we're nice and normal people. I shared a joke with the groom to be by saying that the best part of his wedding would be watching the video in reverse a few weeks after and feeling a sense of relief when he got to the part where he takes his ring off. We clicked instantly. The best man for the wedding was one of the guys Kathy had slept with. 'Gary the git head' he was called, and he was with his girlfriend. I wonder is she knew what I did? I thought I'd keep that little gift-wrapped gem in my think tank for the right moment if required. We all boarded the plane, and once in the air, Kathy and I spent two hundred and forty minutes continuously lying to her friends about our non-existent yet Romeo and Juliet style romantic relationship. For Kathy's sake, and my ordeal to win her back, I reluctantly tried to spark up conversations with Gary the git head and the other toss pot she had slept with, to make her think I was mature, and not the sad pathetic jealous juvenile I was. An air hostess asked me if I wanted anything, so I placed my arm around Kathy and responded, "no thank you I have everything I've ever wanted right here". Kathy had to dig deep to raise a fake smile in front of her friends, and I knew I had to stop playing the fool, as I was less than two weeks away from being dumped on record. If I'd learned anything about Gary the git head on the plane, it was that Kathy liked simpleton bad boys, and I simply didn't possess the skill set or have the acting abilities to live out her fantasy. The most 'bad boy' thing I'd ever done was purchase thirteen items in the ten items or less counter at Sainsbury's. Even then a small log exited my person and into my underwear whilst I was doing it.

After a burdensome flight, we arrived safely in Turkey. The sun was out in full force, so I'd clearly picked the wrong day to build a snowman. Whilst wild cats unashamedly humped each other in every direction, our party headed towards the transfer bus that was taking us to the hotel. There was something about being in a warmer climate that that changed my perception on things, and this was what I was hoping for Kathy with reference to not omitting me from her life. I then stubbed my little toe on the corner of the suitcase trolley, which was surprising pleasant, as I was unaware, that I knew how to River dance. The hotel was an hour drive through some of the ghastliest sights I had ever encountered. And that was just the people. Turkey made Basildon look like the Bahamas. The coach turned into our hotel, and I had a huge sigh of relief. We had driven past some properties that you wouldn't let your worst enemy die in, and our hotel must have been built there by mistake, as it was exquisite and alluring. As we disembarked from the clapped out shed on wheels, we we're greeted by hotel stuff who offered us a complimentary glass of something that looked like champagne. If only it was. It smelled like feet, so I sipped mine down in one and held a mouthful over in case I ever needed to disintegrate a steel structure.

I caught Kathy looking over at Gary the git head in a seductive fashion. I wished she'd have looked at me the same way women would look at new shoes. I was finding it increasing tough to play hard to 'get' because my hard to 'want' game was so strong. We had to wait an hour before we could check into our rooms, so Kathy ordered her favourite sized glass of wine, which was the one that required its own lifeguard. The heat of the sun must have changed Kathy's outlook as she came over to me and said hello when nobody was looking. I was back in the game. We then took a short walk around the resort so we could witness yet more cats performing naughty acts on one another, whilst the fiercely creepy local men stood about dribbling over all the women.

The time arrived for us to check into our room. This was going to be awkward with concerns surrounding sleeping arrangements. I was wishing Kathy and I could sleep in the same bed, however Kathy had other ideas and not so kindly arranged for me to sleep on two chairs pushed together. It was a frustrating pill to swallow, but I was fully aware that if I didn't play by her rules this holiday, I was certain to be spending my next Valentine's day cooking a tantalisingly romantic meal for two in order to enjoy the second plate the following day. With everybody checked into their rooms, our party all descended to the main pool, and got their holidays thoroughly underway. The lads all sampled the heavily watered-down local beer, and the ladies over indulged in their venomous cocktails and toxic wines. Kathy said she couldn't wait to have sex on the beach then expeditiously fled the resort with a box of condoms and returned later in the afternoon arm in arm with three Turkish guys. Kathy was limping and ran straight up to our room for a shower. I asked Kathy how her sex on the beach was and she said it was the best she'd ever had, but I checked the cocktail list and they didn't sell it. I must have just been too thick to see it on the menu. I slowly began losing sight of my goal to win Kathy over when I asked her if we had a chance of rekindling our relationship, and she right away swooped off her sun lounger to a ask random lady at the pool side if her ultra-hot husband was single.

Over the course of the next couple of days, Kathy and I did generate some conversations, and I had a glimmer of hope that I still had time to put things right between us. Even though she treated me badly, I loved her so much, and was prepared to put up with her ways to stay with her. She had gotten so deep into my psyche that I would have never looked at another woman again ever. She was my world. For Kathy, the main perk of dating me was that I laughed at my own jokes, so she didn't have to. We headed into the main restaurant together, and Kathy couldn't decide whether she wanted a screw-top or a cork-based breakfast.

After a few bottles of wine, we relaxed round the pool with the bride and groom to be. The Turkish bar staff ogled Kathy relentlessly, and if I left my sun lounger for more than a whole second, they would parachute over and begin rubbing cream up her legs. It was so desperate and seedy that even the stray cats stopped bonking momentarily to observe the distressing scenes. As the sun rose throughout the course of the day, Kathy spent the afternoon reading a Harry Potter novel, and I continued to find the last Wally on my page. Suddenly a child's scream for help was heard. I turned around to find a young girl drowning in the swimming pool. The lifeguard was busy terrifying holiday makers with the bar staff, so I had no option but to initiate the slow-motion scene from Baywatch and save the day. I dived into the pool, doggy paddled over to the drowning child, and lifted her out of danger to safety. The resort erupted with clapping and cheering. The young girl's parents came over and told me I was arousing, which I already knew, but was nice to hear from somebody other than myself. Our wedding party all congratulated me on being an actual hero, and Kathy felt the opportunity to become famous by expressing compassion and giving me a kiss. In all honesty, I was just pleased that the young girl survived the ordeal, because if she had died, I wouldn't have received the standing ovation I was looking for. The bar staff pulled up their shorts and played 'the Police – illegal alien' for the three hundred and sixty seventh time that day as a thank you to me and gave me a free burger. I played my classic game of food Jenga by removing all the salad bits in the same fashion.

Kathy suddenly acted more human towards me for the next couple of days, and even let me sleep in the bed with her, on the scrupulous condition that if I so much as breathed in her direction, she would sever my body into tiny pieces, put me in a suit case, and throw me into the deepest section of the sea handcuffed to a super colossal sized concrete boulder, then systematically arranged for me to sign a contract to that effect to confirm. I felt she was warming to me again. The following day we attended Kathy's friend's wedding on the beach, and it was a tremendous day. With love in the air and seeing the glow on her friends faces committing to a life time of sharing bills, Kathy suggested we had a small party on the balcony of our hotel room that evening, and of our thirty strong party in Turkey, invited only the two men she had previously slept with. Gary the git head and the other toss pot played cards with Kathy on the balcony, and I pretended to enjoy myself whilst scoffing a jumbo bag of Lays crisps. After a few drinks, the dreaded conversation arose concerning the fact she had slept with them both before. I was trembling with solid rage, as I knew I couldn't say anything, therefore I bit my tongue harder than ever before and taped my mouth up, which was a stupid idea, as I couldn't eat any more crisps. Kathy and the men began reminiscing in a happy way instead of the argumentative and vicious slandering way riddled with tears and recriminations I had hoped for. Gary the git head's girlfriend was sitting around the pool bar, so I decided to join her for a drink. I arrived at the pool bar in my free dressing gown feeling like Hugh Hefner, minus the mansion, the cars, the women, the money, and the magazine, but I had a robe, so it was a start. I perched myself a few stools away from Gary the Git head's girlfriend and ordered a drink. "Can I have the usual please Mustafa?" I softly shouted, and the eerie barman poured me twelve pints of whiskey. I asked Mrs Git head if she wanted to join me, as she was so unattractive, I was never in any doubt that when she tried to jump on me, I would kick her so hard she would land in Greece. She sat next to me, and I entered a conversation by asking her what strategy she had planned to use for stealing all the towels and tea bags from her room on the last day. She slammed thirty liras down next to my drinks and stormed off. Miserable c**t.

I returned to my room, and Gary the Git head had gone, but the other toss pot was still there lurking like a stubborn skid mark. I fell onto the bed and began fake snoring whilst carefully eves dropping and taking extensive notes on every single consonant, vowel, and sound that emulated from the balcony. Eventually the other toss pot departed, and Kathy threw up all over the bathroom floor. I was going to offer to help her clean it up, then sense kicked in and I continued fake snoring. Kathy was then sick again, so I did the decent thing and went in for a poo. Our time in Turkey was over, and during the last couple of days Kathy became exhilaratingly despondent towards me. The impending dumping was alarmingly close now. The moment our feet touched UK soil again, Kathy confirmed my worst nightmare. It was curtains for Jamie and Kathy. She said we were wasting time living a lie, and even when I tried to change the subject by schooling her on the fact that the average parent spends approximately four years and eight months of their lives picking up crayons from underneath restaurant tables, she closed her ears and we separated.

I sobbed my little heart out and moved back in to my Mum's again. I went to the supermarket and loaded the conveyer belt with alcohol to numb the pain. The cashier looked shocked and said, "WOW someone's having a big party", to which I replied "er yeah". I stacked the trolley and sulked back to the car, and I called Kathy in a last-ditch attempt to beg her to give us another go. How she had gotten her claws into me so deep I would never know. She said she couldn't speak as she was on a date and told me never to contact her again, then hung up the phone. I was distraught. She was dating someone else already. I thought the ten second rule only applied to food. I phoned Kathy back just to confirm that she never, ever, ever wanted me to call her again. She confirmed. I got eyeless drunk and made her a cassette tape of me imploring her to take me back. At the time it felt like a good idea, and lumbered round to her flat to post it through her letterbox whilst she was still out on her date. I stood by my decision to do this for years, not realising I'd fallen into the category of 'stupid people'. I was now part of the reason why it was mandatory for manufacturers to write "do not eat" on silica gel packets. I did however think Kathy still has some weird kind of obsession with me, as I found a black sack of photos of us in the bin outside her house. My advice to anybody that is going through anything similar, is that if you love somebody that doesn't love you back, just do the right thing, and set them free, then get blind drunk and text them thousands of times in a row to see if they're seeing anybody else.

CHAPTER 9 - ROBOSLAG

Upon my return to work, I brazenly walked in to the office sun burned and crying. I informed my sympathetic colleagues about my break up and they tried comforting me, but their words left one ear just as quickly as they entered the other. One lady advised me to join the new big social media craze to take my mind off things, and another had a friend they desired to match make me with, but I was years away from being ready to consider a new love interest.

I'd just lost the love of my life. I was missing the cute little things Kathy used to do, like when she pretended not to know me at the cinema and run outside screaming to alert the Police, and date other men etc. She was simply adorable. I refused to let my emotions over rule my intellect and decided to get back into the DJ'ing circuit by joining Essex's most listened to pirate radio station 'Large FM' in 2005. I had played on various but much smaller pirate radio stations since the late 90's, but Large FM was a big deal.

I got in touch with the owner of the station and met up for a drink with him. He was a mostly good lad but could be volatile at times. One minute he might buy you a beer and you'd have a great conversation about old skool music and give money to charity, then the next he would be flipping the studio sofa upside down whilst surging with intolerable anger to reveal a mammoth sized shot gun and would progress to shooting somebody, then go on trial for murder. I loved my time on Large FM, and really helped me trying to forget the upset of Kathy. I had a weekly set with lots of avid listeners, including Greg Fatcheese, Michael Hedgefund, and a high percentage of all the drug dealers in the County. The DJ's and MC's became like family to me and I no longer felt as unimportant as a bald man wearing a golf shirt in a convertible car with a Bluetooth headset in his ear pretending to receive a deal breaking call.

After two years of nil contact with Kathy, I had lost all hope of ever being with her again. We should have been married by now, betting half of my belongings that she'd love me forever. I finally encouraged myself to try dating again, and besides which, I was bored of the desperate lengths Kathy had stooped to by trying to make me jealous, such as marrying her boyfriend and having kids. It was desperately shallow. I found an old used car manual to help me write a dating advert. Once written, I paid for it to be displayed in my local shop window. I went with 'man, white, used, average condition, reliable, cheap, with some evidence of internal damage, seeks any woman'. It couldn't fail. I went on a date with a lady who went to the gym at least twelve times a week, so it became apparent that we both really liked to look after our bodies, because I had recently switched from deep pan to thin crust, however we locked antlers when it came to our music genres. I then met a nice lady sitting next to me on the train to work. She was asleep with her nose pressed against the window, but she turned, and her head fell firmly on to my shoulder and her hair smelled amazing. I speculated as to whether it would be acceptable to wake her up and ask her what shampoo she used, but I didn't wish to appear too impatient, and for the same reason I didn't had said 'hello' to her when she woke up naturally. It did get me thinking that maybe dating somebody unconscious would be ideal for me, but then a lady at my work named Kayleigh Berry reminded me she still had a single friend that would be interested in meeting me. She had made this remark two years earlier, and was referencing the same friend, so there must have been something wrong with her to be single for that long, but I had been single for two years myself, and there was plenty wrong with me. I always felt that if Cupid ever fired an arrow near me, it would hit me in the eye, and I'd bleed to death.

In the end I got in touch with my moral conscience, threw caution to the wind, and told Kayleigh I would meet her unstable friend. Challenge accepted. In a pinch of good fortune, Kayleigh was getting married and I was attending her wedding to which her single friend was also attending, so we decided to meet each other at the wedding, to avoid an unnecessary pressure of an actual first date if we didn't get on, which was likely. At Kayleigh's wedding, I was introduced to her single friend 'Lana Bridgesmell'. To my disappointment, Lana and I got on rather well, and so we agreed to meet up for a proper date. At work the following week, Kayleigh came up to my desk and was gesturing that she was a genius for setting Lana and I up, and how she should be chief bridesmaid when we get married. Kayleigh had become a good friend over the last couple of years, so I really hoped if I did get with her friend, I didn't do anything to ruin it which could cause a rift in my friendship with her. I was exhausted of ordering takeaways every night, then opening the front door when the delivery driver pulled up and shouting back into the house "babe get some plates out, the food has arrived" so they didn't suspect me of being a sad single carb loading female repelling loser. I wanted a relationship again. Kayleigh said that Lana I we're complete opposites, but that opposites always attracted the most. I was looking for someone rich, popular, funny, and happy, so on paper, Lana I would be inseparably magnetic. Lana and I planned to go for a few drinks locally and called me an hour beforehand to advise that she had to urgently baby sit her much younger step brother, who she was planning on taking to the Natural History Museum. I suspected she may have been lying, so I called her bluff by responding "cool, I've always wanted to revisit that place, I'll come with you". Fully anticipating a pretend faulty signal or stuttering, I was shocked when she agreed. That back fired promptly.

I met up with Lana and her step brother then hopped onto the train and headed to the Natural History Museum. Half way into the journey Lana said that I was kind and that I completed her. It worried me immensely, as if I completed her, she must have been missing some disturbing pieces. Lana then received a phone call from one of her friends, and she swiftly remembered that she was in the diary for a girl's day out of drinking. When the phone call ended, Lana bolted up off her seat, and told me that she was going out with her friends to get ridiculously drunk. This could have been my shortest ever date. She then ran to get off the train as it was about to pull out of the station, looked back over her shoulder and said, "hope you both have a nice time, I'll text you my Mum's address so you can drop him off later". Brilliant. I started the day with fire in my belly all excited about meeting a beautiful lady for drinks and banter and potential snogging, yet now I was taking an unknown seven-year-old to a science research centre. This was typical of my luck.

The train doors slammed closed, thus trapping Lana's step brother and I on the train. I tried calling her but we we're travelling underground and had no reception on my phone. I told Lana's brother we we're going to get off the train at the next station and I would take him home, and he cried as he was desperate to go to the museum. I saw the sad look on his little face and couldn't bring myself to deny him the day out he wanted, so I did take him where he wanted to go and made it a fun day for the poor little boy. I bought him lunch, an ice cream, went to the museum, took him on a boat up the River Thames, and he had an enjoyable day. I on the other hand had a vivid glimpse into my future and grew ever more confident that I was going to be a lonely old man on a low budget game show one day that gave a shout out to my cats. After a day of merriment, I returned Lana's step brother to their Mum's house, which wasn't weird having to explain who I was and why I had I'd taken her young child to the Natural History Museum, and I wasn't a sex offender. I went home and slid down a wall in tears, which hopefully burned some calories. I then sat down and watched an advert for a show about an unlovable deadbeat, before realising my TV was switched off, and it was just my reflection on the screen. I put on a DVD and sat back down again. I really needed to find a hobby, as everyone I knew my age was busy enjoying marriages and raising children and being happy, yet I'd just paused 'The little mermaid' to google 'when lobsters die, do they go to heaven?". Out of the blue I received a text message from Lana apologising about what happened and thanked me. She then followed up with a phone call that I hesitantly answered. She was three sheets to the wind, and all I could hear in the background was a pack of her loud friends saying things like "ask him if he wants to take my kids to the Natural History Museum" and "Lana that fit bloke you just got hold of is back from the toilet". I hung up the phone and that was the last time I spoke to Lana Bridgesmell. It did cause a minor hiccup in my friendship with Kayleigh, however I wasn't the one that messed up, so that was a bonus. Kayleigh took me for a burger one lunch by way of an apology for her friends' unforgivable behaviour, which emphasised to me how much of a decent lady she was. If only Lana could have taken a leaf out of Kayleigh's book of morals. Whilst at the restaurant, I saw a stunning lady cuddle her son after he threw some chips on the floor, so I emphatically hurled my entire tray onto the ground. NOTHING!

After a substantial spell of moping around and feeling sorry for myself, a unique distraction presented itself to me, and I needed it. Work had arranged for six employees to do a sky dive on behalf of the firm's charity raising money for disabled children. Being petrified of heights and aeroplanes, I thrust myself into the opportunity and volunteered myself to take part. It was for a worthy cause and would be something new and different I'd never experienced before. I had sponsors approaching me left right and centre, and our firm agreed to match all funds I raised. It was a shame I couldn't raise this money for myself, as I only had enough funds to last me another eleven minutes and couldn't afford to retire until I was three hundred and four. The event was promoted on notice boards, on internal mail to all employees and on social media. There we're a lot of social media sites popping up around this time. The average human could now only survive three weeks without food, three days without water, and three minutes without internet access. I had managed to raise a final tally of over £4,000, so there was no way I could back out of this now, despite being more nervous about it than the time I sneaked a Kit Kat from home into the cinema. On the day of the sky dive I leap frogged out of bed and thought about falling out of an aeroplane at twelve thousand feet with only an eighty square feet sheet of nylon to protect me from certain death.

I psyched myself up, got on the train, and headed up to the airfield. The lady opposite me opened her purse and showed a friend a photo of her son, and they said, "aghhh so cute". Not to be up-staged, I pulled out my two hundred and ninety-five-part accordion wallet photo set of my favourite whiskeys and shoved it into the face of the woman next to me. She poured a bottle of Lucozade over my head and phoned her boyfriend to meet me at the station and put me in a coma. Making new friends was still hard.

CHAPTER 10 – BEER DEATH EXPERIENCE

I reached the airfield and hooked up with the other five lucky guinea pigs that had put their lives on the line to throw themselves out of an aeroplane with me. Four of the five of my fellow air surfers we're cordial colleagues, but one was a jumped-up boisterous whipper snapper, that claimed to have no fear and would be the only one not to have second thoughts once we reached the air. The dive was a tandem, so we we're all buddied up with an experienced sky diver. Everyone seemed to be coupled up with young and strong ex-Army individuals, and I was paired off with a seventy-year-old dwarf.

We boarded the plane and hit the sky. I was feeling a little nervous, but otherwise ok. My back passage began to open wider the higher the plane got, and the loud mouth sprog of the group howled endless amounts of jibber jabber to the group about how we should all be calm like him. I was tempted to cut his parachute chords then strangle him with them. As we reached twelve thousand feet, we were told it was time to jump. I had a sudden reservation and was about to bottle it, when the vociferous embryo of the group got startled by what was about to happen, and the blood rushed from his unlikeable face. This gave me the confidence to continue as planned. I leaned out of the plane, and the guy I was strapped to gave me no warning, just jumped. It was the scariest moment of my life. We were free falling at 180mph. I couldn't breathe. My life flashed before me and random thoughts from the past rushed into my mind, such as 'I can't believe we used to have phones that came attached to a wall' and 'I hope I did my bit to help save the planet when using five gallons of water to rinse out a tiny yoghurt pot for recycling'. As the ground got closer and closer, and quicker and quicker, the little man attached to me opened the parachute at five thousand feet, and it felt like time had stood still. Our descent rate fell dramatically, and the relief of the parachute not failing to open was an emotion of pure elation. The adrenalin zooming around my body was nothing I had ever imagined before. If I lived to tell the tale after this, I was going to have a crazy night ahead of me, by disconnecting the doorbell and eating forty-eight bags of Haribo bears in just my pants. It was going to be unmeasurably mental. Moses may have parted the Red Sea, but I'd jumped out of an aeroplane with all the necessary safety equipment to guarantee my survival and with contingency liability Insurance. Your move bible!

With only a few hundred feet to go until I reached a possible safe landing, I feared a sudden wind would divert me into an active volcano, but no, the little man on my back had done it. I landed safely with all limbs in the same place they were an hour earlier. Success! After a rollercoaster of emotions, I was alive and well, and raised a shed load of cash for disabled kids. I'd never felt prouder of myself. The rowdy lamebrain went ahead with his jump and landed moments after me, which was a shame. We shook hands, gathered up our parachutes and headed back to the front desk. Until today, my greatest achievement in life had been winning an egg and spoon race aged six (by default (long story)), and now this. Dreams can come true my friends. Our team of six had all successfully completed out jumps and congregated for a publicity photo in our company branded clobber. We then headed to the local pub for lunch before going our separate ways. I tricked one of them into buying me a free Surf N Turf by saying "you get this, and I'll pay next time", then resigned from the Company, ignored them forever, and made a brand-new circle of friends.

CHAPTER 11 - SQUIRTER

In 2009 I sought pastures new and appeared at my new Company performing a similar role to that of my previous employer, only back in London and for more money. I was hoping for more simi-lar minded colleagues like those at my previous job. I never asked for much for much in life, except to be able to buy whatever I wanted, whenever I wanted it, always and forever, without my bank account ever deducting any of the money I ever spent, and some friendly work colleagues. I made a new best friend at the firm named Jamarn Pillwomen. She was great for entertainment value but would often wet herself if she laughed too much, inter-mittently I might add, just squirts here and there.

The best thing about the new job was that a woman came into our office every morning with sandwiches, so we didn't have to burn unnecessary calories using our own legs to walk outside. Pay rises and pension contributions we're also important, but hey, Ham and Cheese sandwiches delivered to your hand. Priceless! Every-body in the office knew when the sandwich lady (dubbed Picnic Patricia) arrived as Jamarn acting as a human fire alarm, by char-ging over first to the boxes of food first, leaving a trail of squirts behind her. Jamarn would typically purchase ninety percent of the sandwiches leaving the other fifty employees fighting over the last remaining BLT or starving to death. I often wondered how she ate forty odd sandwiches per day, but if I got my honey roast ham, I didn't care. There we're some really attractive ladies on our floor, but if ever I asked them if they fancied having a bath with me, they would always respond "sorry you're not my type" which I soon learned means "he is perfect in every way, but there is noth-ing about him that would make other girls jealous if I had him". One morning I was sitting at my desk watching hardcore pornog-raphy with the headphones on, and everybody started looking at me funny. I removed the headphones but could still hear all the professional tennis noises. I'd forgotten to plug the headphones in, and my computer was cranked up to maximum volume. I wasn't allowed to watch sex videos during core production hours after that, not because of the headphone's incident, but I became too invested in the storylines, and always ended up worrying as to whether the plumber ever lost his job for taking too long. Oh, and management having given me a written warning. On one morning, Picnic Patricia was late, and when she did finally arrive, I found a pubic hair in my sandwich. I didn't find it amusing, but Jamarn was squirting all over the ceiling. Anyway, I did the most logical thing possible, by cello taping the hair to an extra strong mint and posting it via internal mail to one of my colleagues in another office. Somebody was about to think Christmas had come early!

Jamarn worked with a man named Jamie Pantsoff and she introduced me him. I wasn't happy we shared the same first name, nevertheless he was hilarious, and looked like the comedian Sean Lock. He was a real bad boy that knew exactly how to talk to women with confidence and ease. Monday's were usually the most prominent time for me to consider committing suicide, but in this office, if Jamarn and Jamie Pantsoff were not on holiday, I could cement myself to my chair and be certain of a good day. Jamie Pantsoff would tell us stories about some of the women he had met at the weekend and describe how he boxed clever by not doing what other men would say or do which women found often predictable and boring. He would ask women for their email address instead of their name, pretend to be an off-duty pilot, or ask them if they wanted tickets to watch him work out on his arms and neck. The man was an inspiration for somebody like me. At lunch times he would eat spaghetti bolognaise with his hands. I sat in a corner of four with Jamarn, Jamie Pantsoff, and a lady named Ribena Cortina. I spent the entire day laughing with them all until we we're blue in the face or I got another written warning, or I choked on a pubic hair.

Out of nowhere, the formidable foursome was about to be broken up, as our company required some individuals to travel to India for a couple of months to kick start a new team of off-shore trainee's. Banks and other technology-based entities had been doing for some time, but now it was our time to outsource work to save the Company money and ultimately to put ourselves out of employment. Within just three months, customers would be able to contact our Company, be put on hold for three days whilst listening to a flute solo and be told that their call was important to us. Flying half way across the World to another continent to work for an elongated period wasn't for everyone due to personal commitments, the language barrier, and the mental stamina required to see it through to completion and was fair enough. All I had depending on me in life was a house plant, which I was pretty sure was dead anyway. Being devoid of all human emotion by this stage, the only sensation I had left was the burning agony on the roof of my mouth from when I got an apple pie from McDonalds back in 1997 and ate it too quickly. That pain never left me. I was going to grasp this fortuitous break and make a success of it. Besides the sky dive, I'd achieved nothing noteworthy, besides having one single eyebrow hair that somehow grew up to five inches long overnight, and possibly being able to find the flame emoji on my phone in under fifteen minutes. Whilst I added my name into the hat for a place on the India business trip, I was saddened that Jamarn, Jamie Pantsoff, and Ribena had not put themselves forward. Low and behold, I was accepted as one of the five individuals, and would heading to India in a months' time. I had three other excellent colleagues coming with me, and one not so much.

I went home that evening with a broader than broad smile. I stopped at my local shop who were handing out free samples of Swiss Winter and mixed berry smoothies. I guzzled one down and the man that offered it to me asked me if I liked it. I replied, 'berry much so', and struggled to breathe whilst roaring with laughter. He said I wasn't funny, so he must have been a bit slow or allergic to comedy, and I told him to 'Swiss off'. I was on form that day, and suspect the guy was bent double with laughter the next day when he got the joke. I began packing for my trip to India, safe in the knowledge that soon I would be jetting away and getting my head straight whilst achieving what was going to be an uphill and stressful challenge. I would no longer be surrounded by things that made my blood curdle such as couples that celebrate their three-month anniversary like it's an achievement, when I'd had plates in my sink for longer than that, and not being worried about how I will be able to afford food for remaining twenty-nine days until payday. My financial status was in tatters. As a child I feared the dark, but with overdue electricity bills sitting on my dining room table, I had become scared of the light. Work arranged for my visa to be issued and I had a cocktail of injections to allow me to fly, which reacted beautifully with my body, leaving me curled up in a ball of affliction for a week. I consumed a whole bottle of brandy to bring down the pain, then woke up on the kitchen floor and found my TV remote, a pillow, five shoes, and my dead plant in the fridge. It's amazing that society allowed me to live by myself. With everything now in place, I was ready to leave the UK.

CHAPTER 12 – THE HATE ESCAPE

The day had finally arrived for me to fly away. I went into the office with my suitcase link up with my colleagues and pulled a cup out of the work dishwasher for one last cup of British tea for a couple of months. The cup had a lipstick mark on the side, but I didn't change it. I used it for my tea and counted it as a snog. I wasn't a lonely in the slightest. Jamarn let me have the last Honey Roast pubic hair sandwich that day, and then it was time to depart. As I walked past the female toilets, a lady from another team exited on her mobile phone and said to the recipient "then I set my vibrator to F5 Tornado mode and held onto the door for sheer life". I'll never forget that moment, as I noticed she was wearing a fashionable designer watch, and I like a classy lady.

Along with my other four colleagues, we stepped into the taxi and briskly travelled at snails' pace to the airport. We checked in and headed directly to the VIP lounge to drain expenses. At passport security I was asked if I was carrying any guns, so I tensed my arms and said, 'do these bad boys count?'. Not everybody has a sense of humour let me assure you, and strip searches aren't fun! The eldest member of our group 'Chief Bathroom' became my adopted Dad for the foreseeable future, and was a heavy smoker dreading the ten-hour flight ahead without a cigarette, so he drank three pints of Tia Maria in half an hour to help relax him before lift-off. I knew I'd met my kindred spirit. My Mum always told me that 'alcohol is your enemy', but Jesus said 'thou shalt love thy enemy', and I wasn't good with mixed messages, so I just drank everything I could see. Across the bar I spotted Nicola, Billy Lightswitch, and Roxanne Beachballhead and they all noticed me. I could have really done without seeing them. Being the bigger person, I decided to say hello to them. Roxanne said they were heading to the USA and Billy said they we're off to USSR. I explained that the Soviet Union collapsed in 1992, but Billy laughed and choked on a party sausage. Common sense is not a gift, it's a punishment, because you must deal with everyone else that doesn't have any. Some things never changed. Twenty years ago, I bought four turtles and a rat, then released them into a sewer. Every day I visited them and slid a pizza into the drain, but nothing ever happened. I knew I was cursed. I wished them well, and they made their way to the boarding gate for a flight to Ibiza.

Chief and I headed to our gate and after some delays, we we're on board the airbus taking us to another continent. A beautiful air hostess asked me if she could get me anything, and I advised I wanted her height, weight, and body mass index, so that I could calculate the amount of alcohol she would need to make her think I was sexy. She never bothered me again. We hurtled down the runway and began our journey to paradise. Chief was shaking being tobacco deficient and rolled up an on-board drinks menu to pretend to smoke. The plane was full of friendly people all chin wagging with each other except me. You'd be surprised at how many strangers will let me hug them when I approached with open arms and a big smile. NONE. That's how many. Half way into the flight we experienced severe turbulence. One of my many greatest fears was being stuck inside a giant tin can and nosing diving into a cliff face at 500mph with only a flimsy lap belt to protect me. It wouldn't be half as bad if planes we're fitted with air bags full of confetti to make accidents more fun. If the plane crashed, I might have been sad that I'd just lost my legs, but then suddenly I'd be all 'hey a party', then die happier. Thankfully the bad weather passed, and we landed safely in Bangalore. Although it was late at night, the temperature was still soaring. Chief ran out of the airport and smoked thirty cigarettes in one hand at once. A smoke cloud formed around him as if he was going to burst out with a microphone and perform a Barry White number.

We met our driver 'Nryan' and proceeded to our hotel. Nryan didn't speak one word of English, and I didn't speak one word of

Hindi. We had some great chats. Through the method of a made-up sign language and scribbling down lots of drawings, we broke through the language barrier and he never once let us down. His punctuality was impeccable. The hotel was far greater than I had envisaged. I had anticipated something like my old Lego house, nevertheless it was plentifully plush. We had swimming pools, a top-notch bar, exquisite rooms, and toilet paper. We all ditched our suitcases in our rooms and sprinted back to the hotel bar for last orders. The bar man 'Atul' spoke very good English, so we began drinking excessively whilst being nurtured on the local area. Every unit of alcohol consumed takes a minute off your life, and I'm no Pythagoras, but according to my calculations I died in 214 BC, but this was a once in a life time adventure, therefore embraced it. After a hurried session, we went to settle our bill. We we're told that we had a small and limited budget per day for essential items, which we had to pay up front and then claim back on expenses later, but Atul showed us an email advising we could have whatever we want and to add it to a tab for the Company to collect direct. My eyes burst out of their sockets. Chief was one step ahead of me and was already retrieving his eye balls from the floor. Chief pointed to a strong box behind the bar and began adding £250 exported Cuban cigars to our tab. It would have been great if I could have traded my heart in for another liver, that way I could have drank more and cared less. This was going to be a grubby trip, as I wasn't an alcoholic, but enjoyed celebrating absolutely everything.

The next day we were due to meet our Team of delegates in the Bangalore office. Nryan had slept in his car outside our hotel over night to ensure he wasn't late picking us up, and we left our five-star super luxury hotel to tour past poverty and sin and be greeted by our new office and team for the next couple of months. The building was over eight stories high, and basic health and safety hadn't been invented yet in India, as employees would have their lunch on its flat roof with no barriers. I had a hangover that felt like Quentin Tarantino had directed it, and appeared that paracetamol, Tuna, white bread, and drinkable tea bags were a very distant pipeline dream for this Country. My thought process had shifted from lusting over an ex to being sexually attracted to ASDA. Us trainers were assigned a team of seven people each, so we took our teams to one side to get to know each other. My team we're the loveliest people I had ever met, consisting of four men that three young ladies. I listened to what little of their words I understood and spent the remainder of the time on Google madly searching for a place that sold tea bags and sedatives locally. I'd have settled for a whale tranquiliser given the pounding surrounding my brain. With the first day of introductions and system checking complete, we all headed back to the hotel to laboriously jam our bodies full of Company paid alcohol. The best way to reboot my body was CTRL ALT and BEER. I returned to my room to get changed and entered the bar three minutes later to find Chief finishing off a tray of flaming sambuca's whilst nine absurdly overpriced cigars burned away in his ears.

Chief and I bonded further over a bottle of champagne and became acquainted with our new joint number one enemy at the bar. Allow me to introduce Jim. Where to start with this clown. He was an Irish man in his 40's that was living off his poor wife's salary. We never met his wife, but the story was that she had been seconded from the UK to earn mega money in India, whilst Jim spent the entire day and night spending her hard-earned money at the bar. He was permanently drunk and delivered endless stories riddled with loopholes as to how hard, popular and clever he was. Chief had a short fuse at the best of times, so I was worried about his temper, as Jim solemnly infuriated me from the first second of meeting him. After another barrel of sambuca's, Chief and I retired for the evening, and Jim somehow managed to survive witnessing another day. He truly was a septic spot on the back side of humanity. I had been blessed that when growing up my Mum never allowed me to play computer games due to their violent nature, and instead forced to play family friendly board games containing questions such as, 'who murdered Colonel Mustard with a pipe in the conservatory?', otherwise I'd have prevented Jim from breathing again that evening. If I was ever about to be murdered, I'd ask the murderer to hold on for a moment, in order to put on an octopus costume, because those people that draw a chalk outline around the victim's bodies have such a boring job. I'm nice like that.

The next few weeks were mentally draining. My four colleagues and I had been working fourteen-hour days and struggled to train our teams to an acceptable standard. We were well behind the projected curve, and the hangovers were becoming even more unbearable as a result of the long hours in the office, then having to throw as many units of alcohol down our necks as we could before closing time at the bar. The only benefits to this were that my dark emotional thoughts we're slowly lifting, I was saving a ton of cash on booze, and Irish Jim had usually passed out by the time we got to the bar of an evening. Chief had been inspirational in helping me improve my outlook on life with his decades of wisdom and late-night tipsy chats. He was a luminary. He could also have been a millionaire if had contacted live bands that couldn't afford smoke machines, as he'd have stood in front of them in exchange for a few cartons of Benson and Hedges and exceeded all expectations for free.

Our project had been scheduled for two months based on five trainers, however two of my colleagues had to go home early and one had a nervous breakdown, leaving only Chief and I. This meant the timeframe had to be extended by a couple of months if Chief and I agreed to it. With the price of beer rocketing in London, Chief and I agreed to stay on, and we worked our socks off to get our teams to the required specification. Successfully completing the project was back within our remit, so we headed to the bar to mastermind some new obscure cocktails, when we overheard a lady with an accent from my local area ordering wine.

Being three thousand miles from home and hearing an Essex accent behind you is a real head turner. I was never the best at sparking up conversations with women, so I very hastily killed a wasp and glued it to my hand, then sneaked up behind her and said "watch out there's a wasp" then gently slapped her back with the wasp free hand and show her the dead wasp in the other. My introduction was spot on and the lady began undressing me with her eyes before saying "don't you ever touch me again". After Chief had diffused the situation, and the lady had addressed herself as 'Glenda' to him, we all had a chat, and it evolved that she lived not too far from me and was working on the floor above Chief and I in the Bangalore office. If this wasn't a sign of fate from God, then I didn't know what was. We plied her with a new cocktail Chief, and I had invented called 'Jamie's Bathroom'. It was basically half tequila and part vodka with a dash of Cinzano and a secret ingredient only found in window cleaner, not forgetting an ice cube for taste. After ten litres each of the cocktail, we we're relatively joyous. Glenda then introduced us to her much taller, much fitter, much richer, much smarter, and significantly more well-endowed than me boyfriend. I wasn't sceptical. Glenda and her boyfriend Marty became part of our after-work gatherings, and to be honest, they were a cool couple, unlike Irish Jim whose life I still wanted to terminate. I couldn't dance to save my life, but when Sambuca told me I could, I complied with its request quicker than Glena had time to run away.

Having been in India for three months, I became accustomed with some of the very different ways of life, learned a few Hindi and Tamil words, made some life long friends, and the work project was an astronomical success thanks principally to Chief and I. We had to make one final conference call back to the UK with our peers, and in a few days time we would be getting back on the plane after quarter of a year away from home. Conference calls were great if you just wanted to hear fifteen or so people say "what?" from the bottom of a well, but they weren't for me. Our peers congratulated us both on the fantastic achievement we had seen through to the end by successfully off shoring some work under challenging conditions with endless obstacles placed in our path, but finally, the task was over. Chief and I hoped for a sub-stantial bonus for taking over one hundred days out of our lives to travel half way around the world to work fourteen-hour days for our company to make a renowned gold mine whilst jeopardising our own careers, but instead we got a week free gym membership. We were livid. The only time I'd ever set foot in a gym was to use the vending machine when the one in our works kitchen broke, and I never wanted to go to the gym anyway, in case I got out of breath and somebody asked me to play a saxophone straight after-wards. It wouldn't have been so degrading if they had bought me a treadmill as at least I'd have something to hang my clothes on. Chief and I didn't protest too much as our bar tab wasn't due to be settled until the day we left, and rumour had it the total sum had already exceeded Bill Gates net worth. Chief and I had been screwed. I asked Atul at the bar if he could add fifteen thousand pounds in Rupees to my bar tab so I could throw it into a wishing well, and wish I was better with money. On our last evening in India, Chief and I met up with Glenda and Marty and had a compe-tition as to who could spend the most of our Company's money. We lined up all the champagne on the bar, smoked all the cigars from the strong box, and insisted that Glenda and Marty have whatever they wanted on Chief and I. It was a crazy night. Cham-pagne was the leading cause for me dancing to the greatest hits of the Prodigy like a new born deer in high heels. I stood outside the bar trying to convince patrons inside that I was shrinking, by walking backwards and forwards past the window with progres-sively larger jars of Turmeric. Glenda was galvanized by my sharp wit and considered ditching Marty for me by the time I'd located the largest jar.

The evening went on into the early hours of the morning and hav-ing been such good customers at the hotel bar, Atul agreed to keep the bar open all night for us, despite not having much left to sell. We hadn't spent enough money yet, and were determined to fin-ish everything they had, even if we had to be at the airport in a few hours' time. Nryan was sleeping in the back of his car at the hotel car park, so we lifted as many crates of the costliest champagne we could find into the boot for him and his wife to enjoy, then bought him a new car. Atul put my drum and bass CD on at full volume as the only other people in the bar besides our crowd was a deaf man, who I gave a thumbs up to every time I yawned so he knew I was screaming. Marty collapsed face down in a washing up bowl full of caviar I imported for him, and Chief was in a corner hiding behind the smoke of a bush fire. Glenda and I big toe skanked to the music whilst devouring limited edition magnums of exported Johnny Walker.

At last, we had finally drunk everything the bar had to offer. I shouldn't have been alive at this point. Chief and I had five minutes until Nryan came in and took us to the airport, so I furiously wrapped up all the bar stools, and posted them to my home address on my tab. The competition was almost over, and I had beaten Chief by one rupee. I was exultant to have won. Nryan came into the hotel bar to resuscitate us, and Chief suddenly appeared from behind the bar hugging a pile of floorboards he had lifted, and went outside to burn them in order to add the material damage to his tab. He'd only gone and beaten me an inch from the finish line. Sneaky b*stard. I knew he would. Glenda asked me to perform the jar trick one last time, so I did, and she became exorcised. She shattered an iron bar into my knee caps then straddled me as I tried to crawl away. "You're not going anywhere until your weapon has leaked in my ovaries" she shrieked. Chief removed the demon from my person, and Nryan fashioned together a wheelchair using empty bottles and cigar ends to get me to the car. Nryan and Chief placed me in the car, and we annoyingly screeched out of the car park and headed to the airport. Nryan stopped for petrol and I asked him if could get a tuna sandwiches with white bread if they had any, but I don't think he understood my drawing properly, as he came back with a manhole cover and last of the summer wine on VHS. We waved Nryan goodbye and Chief plonked me in a suitcase trolley to wheel me to check in. I got stopped at the security scanner for marginally breaching the one hundred millilitres of liquid rule in my hand luggage. I only had six litres of champagne in my back pack and pleaded with the guard to let me through. After a brief discussion, we came to a compromise, and the security man took all six bottles of champagne and all the cash in my wallet from me, in exchange for keeping my life. I tell you what, I drove a hard bargain.

I'd somehow made it onto the plane with the assistance of Chief and collapsed in my seat clutching my knee caps. I asked an air hostess for the Wi-Fi password and she replied, "not now I'm doing the safety demonstration". I advised her that seemed too long for a password and enquired as to whether it was all in lower case. I sat next to a fellow Brit and we began chatting. I told him how betrayed I felt by my Company when they offered me an insulting weeks gym pass for all my hard work. He was thinking of joining a gym himself as he wanted to impress his girlfriend and asked me what I thought was the best machine to use. I suggested the cash machine then enjoyed almost half a Day of uninterrupted Silence. The closer we got to the UK, the more existential anxiety overruled my body. It was time to face the negative reality of constant reminders of my past on every corner whilst almost certainly being on crutches for a few weeks. Although I had initial concerns about going to India, I didn't want to return home. I almost heaved. The fear and alcohol cocktail marinating inside me felt it necessary to try and leave my body. I rushed to the cock pit end of the plane and locked myself in the toilet. After an hour I headed back to my seat, and Instead of getting annoyed with me, the unknown lady reading her book at the front of the plane should have simply thanked me for taking the initiative to remove the tweezers from her handbag and selflessly pluck out her unruly ear hairs. Ungrateful wasn't even the word.

The seat belt light came on, and we were ready to land. I looked out of the window to be greeted by grey clouds and heavy rain. I needed to feel as excited as I was when I was a child, when huddled round the radio on a snowy morning with my Mum, listening to the DJ announcing an endless list of schools closed for the day, then after an hour eventually hearing my school being read out, and fist punching the air all the way to my sledge. Within minutes we had landed safely, and I hobbled off my seat. I spotted Mick Jagger a few rows in front of me, so I hopped over and asked him for an autograph. Unfortunately, it was just a dispirited grandma called Barbara and her husband wanted to deck me. I made quite a few new friends on that flight. I phoned my Mum to let her know I had landed safely, and she replied, "oh have you been away?".

I collected my luggage, said goodbye to Chief, and limped out to the taxi rank to return home. I clambered into the cab and commuted to my house. It was raining outside and 'it's raining men' came on the radio. The irony. Why did it always have to rain men? Why couldn't it rain something useful like mortgage payments or whiskey? I rang Greg Fatcheese and a few others from the back of the cab to let them know I was back. Greg suggested we go out and have a mad weekend to celebrate. I didn't understand people who did things at the weekend. You just did things all week! What next? MORE things? Upon returning home, I used a system of weights and pullies to get myself upstairs and began unpacking.

As I glanced out the window, I noticed my neighbours setting up a new six-foot swimming pool in their garden. I had a feeling I'd be in that during the early hours of Saturday morning, but I only had two days until I was back at work and had to sober up from my four months nonstop binge. My neighbours then started having a major argument, so to assist the ambience, I grabbed an enormous speaker and played tragically sad love songs on repeat at my wide-open window, because everybody deserved a little ice breaking background music during a savage break up. I thought I was helping, but some people are weird, as Tyler and Mandy certainly didn't seem to think so. I grabbed some micro sleep and then went to the hospital to get my legs fixed, followed by a visit to the works private surgery for a mandatory return to England check-up. The Doctor asked me if I was sexually active, and I advised her I wasn't even physically active. She didn't give me a high five or anything. How rude?

CHAPTER 13 – STRESSED TO IMPRESS

Monday morning, and I had to return for my first day back in the office since India. I rose more and more tense and edgy about going back to work, like when you accidently heart an ex's selfie on social media, then your palms sweat, and your heart flies out of your chest, and you want to kill yourself. As I faltered over to my team, they all cheered and cried and hired the Red Arrows to spray 'we missed and love you Jamie' into the sky. Jamarn went into the kitchen and trickled back with a lukewarm tea for me. I had a chat with Ribena Cortina and caught up on Jamie Pantsoff's most recent tales of lust. I had really missed these people.

I was still a tad queasy from all the alcohol in my system, so I blamed the food, and told the team I needed to go and be sick and maybe have a poo to kill two birds with one stone. The men's toilet only had one cubical and the door appeared locked. I pushed it gently open as it was unlocked, however I was met by a sad guy with no phone. I was in shock. Imagine accidentally walking in on someone using the toilet who is not messing around on their phone, just sitting there, hands on their lap, like some sort of medieval psychopath. I told him I was in a hurry and he could see by the colour of my cheeks that I wasn't bluffing, and kindly left me to lose weight fast. A new lady called 'Arsenal Pasta' had joined our team whilst I had been jet setting. She seemed cool and fit, and we became friends.

I spent the next few months sat at home alone against the living room radiator drinking Jack Daniels every evening. I told my new friend Arsenal and she said I had a problem. It was nice to have a new friend to reduce to tears about stories of my failed relationships. Arsenal took pity on me and listened to my worries. She told me that my future girlfriend was probably texting her current boyfriend telling him how much she loved him. I settled back in again at work, and slowly developed a life by joining another pirate radio station, doing a charity bike ride in a mankini along Southend sea front, and even tried shedding a few lbs. The secret to losing weight is knowing what your triggers are and then avoiding them, and my trigger was eating food.

Felling better about myself I was ready to delve into the dating spectrum again. I lied and told Arsenal I had a date lined up and she was ecstatic for me. Any night can be a date night if you sit close enough to a stranger at the Odeon cinema in Southend. I thought me and orange dress girl made a lovely couple. Before I went to India, I briefly met a stunning lady at a friend's birthday party who had a boyfriend, so I only exchanged a few words with her at the time, and thought nothing of it, as I would probably never see her again, and if I did, she'd hate me, but I did see her again. I spotted her in a club, but wasn't entirely sure if it was her, as I'd only seen her once, and it was over a year ago. She recognised me and came over to say hello. She was still beautiful, and I couldn't see her boyfriend anywhere close. Not to seem over eager, I played it cool by googling 'how many Twiglets would it take to build a raft capable of carrying a dog past the end of Southend pier' then telling her the answer as she acknowledged me. If Google ever went down permanently, I would be screwed, as I only knew four other facts which all about goldfish, and I'd already forgotten three of them. I guessed there was somebody standing behind me that she liked and was talking to them, but no, she intentionally spoke to me without a gun to her head, and it wasn't for a bet. I casually enquired about the whereabouts of her boyfriend, so as not to over step the fine line of making her think I was scarily interested in her, but also to confirm that I wasn't gay on the off chance she was drunk enough to like me for a second. She said she had split up with him and the jackpot symbol scrolled round my eye balls.

Her name was 'Dani Docks' and it was now more important than ever that I did not say or do anything stupid. "So, do you eat hair?"

I asked Dani. My brain must have required an update, as I didn't know where those words came from, yet within ten seconds of talking to Dani, I had lavishly abolished any chances of me ever talking to her again. To my amazement Dani was laughing. She thought I was being funny instead of the doapy senseless dummy I was. I asked her if she would ever go on a date with me during our current life times, and she said yes. I thought I was in a dream, only not the recurring one where I am an archaeologist in the future digging up sun beds and assuming that previous generations were fried for punishment. Even if Dani hated me, going on a date was a win-win situation, because if things went well, we would eat food and fall in love, and if she climbed out of the toilet window to marry the first person she set eyes on, I'd still get to eat food, and that's all that really matters. I took her number, and we parted ways for the evening without her having to call the Police, which was a big step forward for me. Finally, I had a real date to tell Arsenal about rather than confusing loneliness for desperation then lying about it again.

I was giddy with excitement as I had an actual real date with Dani Docks on the cards. We had arranged to meet at a local Italian restaurant in a few days' time, and amidst out interim text communication, she revealed that she had heard me playing on the radio, and thought I was barely listenable. That was the biggest compliment I had been given to date. Maybe all my failed relationships had helped me finally understand women. All they wanted was everything, but nothing, and all at the same time or different times, sometimes but not always. Why did I not get this sooner? On the day of the big first date, I met Dani in her local high street, so we could go for a drink before the meal. She lived in quite a rough area, as I remembered a time when wearing pyjamas outside meant your house was on fire, but it was fashionable round her way. Thankfully Dani did not dress like the others, and she arrived looking more beautiful than anything I could ever describe. We shared a bottle of wine, and I fleetly learned we liked the same music, comedy, and films, and she ticked all the boxes I could think of. After a good chat, it was time to go to the restaurant. I behaved like a gentleman by holding the door open for her, but Dani insisted she could go into the cubical by herself, and once she'd had a little tinkle, we left the pub and were on our way for some food. The night had started out so well that I thought soon I may have been able to stop shouting "wait for me guys" whenever I was in public so that everyone thought I have friends.

Dani and I were shown to our table, and our free-flowing and congenial conversation promoted. They say you learn something every day, and on this day, I discovered that olives are delicious if you love the taste of drowning at sea. After a few more glasses of wine, my bladder had reached its topmost capacity, and so I went to deflate. Going to the toilet during a date is risky, as I'd learned that women's minds begin to wander, and they got thoughts such as 'what am I doing here?', 'should I just leave now?', and 'oh my ex has text me a generic template I must get back with him tonight' etc. I took my phone off the table as it was common knowledge that the fastest land animal was a woman that sees a man's phone light up and feels the urge to fly over and trawl through it. I tried to wee as snappily as possible before any thoughts entered Dani's brain. I was so afraid of this happening that I saved half of it for later. To my consternation, I returned to find Dani not just still in the restaurant, but also at the same table. I wasn't interested in being a billionaire, I just wanted exactly this. A beautiful lady that didn't run away from me, and possibly enough money to be able to stare into the distance whilst filling my car up with petrol. I had a hunch I had finally met one of the rare good ones, and that I'd never be so sad again that I wouldn't be forced into the downward spiral of liking a cream cheese page on social media again. Dani was everything I had ever wished for, because the panic of thinking of things to say to her distracted me from the anxiety of being alive.

The date came to an end and I debated steaming in for a kiss, but I didn't want to let her think I was an abnormal monster, so I shook her hand and said, "pleased to meet you". She pushed away my hand and gave me a snog. It was impeccable. Chateau nerf de pap became my new favourite aphrodisiac. I waited for Dani to get into a cab and then made my own way home. I tried sending Dani a nice long thank you text but autocorrect amended the kiss face emoji to 'for God sake you're thirty-two years old' and switched my phone off. I got home pumped with happiness, and my neighbours began listening to drum and bass music for seven hours straight, because that's what I played.

The next day I went into work with an illuminated smile, and I told Jamarn, Jamie Pantsoff, Ribena, and Arsenal about my night. Being visibly on Cloud 9, they knew it went well before I'd even flicked through my first fifty pages of notes. They we're all so pleased that I'd finally been on a first date that didn't begin or end with her sleeping with someone else. Arsenal was dubious of this and warned me to stay grounded. I knew she had my best interests at heart, but I had completed a date with a human being that didn't go completely wrong. For the next few months, Dani and I were inseparable, barring twice a week when she would stay at the same single unknown male's house, who she claimed was a lifelong friend that she met after we started dating which was less than ninety days ago. Then Dani dropped some bad news. She had been offered a job in Ghana which she was likely to accept. I couldn't believe my luck. I had met the perfect lady and therefore the logical design for the next part of my life was to relocate her seven hours away on another continent. Dani was in two minds whether to go as I think a tiny part of her either liked or felt sorry for me, and a part of her brain wasn't function properly. Dani gave herself a week to decide what she was going to do before committing one way or the other. When we met each other during this spell, we couldn't have fun properly, as the ticking time bomb was looming over us. I was experiencing the same feelings I had towards the end with Kathy. My stomach made weird noises, so I sent eight Big Mac's down to check it out, and even that didn't help. I kept telling myself that if I was half an inch taller, and maybe a lot less weird, and had a bigger heart, and had a different face, and was younger, and much richer, she would stay. Arsenal very kindly took time out of her busy day to help try and take some of the pain away, but it was like trying to take a fish off a wild bear.

On day seven of Dani's ultimatum, I text her off the hook all day asking if she wanted to meet up and let me know her decision. I did feel terrible putting pressure on her, but I was super anxious to know where I stood. She sent me a text at the end of the day saying 'sorry I've only just seen all your texts and haven't responded as I've been excessively busy chasing a cherry tomato around my plate with a fork. I almost had it about an hour back. Just need a little longer babe. Thanks for your patience." The lack of acknowledgement on the topic in hand spoke volumes, and as for the tomato thing, well, she could have been telling the truth, so I gave her benefit of the doubt and waited patiently with my fists clenched. Jamarn and Arsenal both advised me that Dani was legging me up. My phone began playing the final countdown tune, and it was Dani calling. I answered the call, and I could sense by the way she opened the call that it wasn't going to be the news I wanted to hear. Then she hit me with it. She was going to move to Ghana. My heart attended its own funeral. This could only happen to me.

Dani then asked me if I would go with her. Maybe she didn't hate me one hundred percent or more. I would have done absolutely anything to be with her, except go to Ghana, not that. The dream was over before it had even begun, as she was off in a few days' time. Contact with Dani was minimal over the next few days, and I put everything on the line and pleaded with her not to go, but her mind was set, and before I had time to say goodbye properly, she had gone, and history had repeated itself. I was so depressed I bought an adult colouring in book.

CHAPTER 14 – SUPER WHORE

After a few days of Dani's departure, I was still in bits, and decided to do some exercise to feel a bit more upbeat. I purchased an exercise mat, and my bank immediately cancelled my card because they deemed it to be suspicious activity on my account, then Dani called me crying. She said she missed me and really wanted me to come to Ghana, which, to reiterate, was the very last place on the planet I ever wanted to go. Dani assured me it wouldn't be a waste of my time flying out there for a week to see what I though of the place, but I'd rather have swallowed a rusty knife than go there.

Maybe I was being a bit too hasty and selfish. I really liked her, and so I agreed to go. Dani and I we're both so happy about the development. I rushed through a visa and booked in for a yellow fever injection. Jamarn, Jamie Pantsoff and Ribena Cortina said I may have been rushing into things, but I blinkered by love. Arsenal didn't mix her words when she told me Dani was a slag, and I loved her honesty, but at the time, if Dani told me to set my legs on fire that day, I'd have jumped into a swimming pool of petrol with lit fireworks strapped to my shins. Dani was house sharing with a direful Lebanese man who allowed me to stay there for the week. Dani and I spoke every day and revitalised our connection. On the day of my yellow fever injection at a private clinic, I had the jab, and left the building to enter an adverse reaction which left my arm paralysed. I went home and laid in bed with a death-defying headache, and I was in world of pain for the next few days. This was worse than the injections I had before I went to India, or the time I decided to give up alcohol for a day and I heard the Mission Impossible theme tune playing in my head. I couldn't work out why my body was so weak. I was usually so fit and strong. A few weeks prior to this event, a friend tried to pull me onto the dancefloor when I was still sober and so I resisted so hard he ended up floating through twelve windows. I was seriously considering cancelling going to Ghana, but if I did, that would be it for Dani and I and she would not invite me back again, even if I thought Ghana did smell like Brussels sprouts and pound shop deodorant. I had to get well fast. Arsenal tried to convince me to stay and advised me there were plenty of fish in the sea and would even hook me up with one her friends instead. As loving and caring and loyal as Arsenal has been to me, I told her that there were also dangerous sharks, oil spills, plane wreckage, and Somalian pirates in the sea. It was basically like saying there's plenty more water in the toilet.

I went out to get some soup, as whenever someone is ill they always have soup and then get better, like 'I have flu', eat soup, cured, 'my stomach feels poorly', eat soup, cured, 'I've got aids', eat soup.....well, you get the point. I located the section in my local supermarket and expected to find roughly three different flavours of the stuff, but oh no, there were rows and rows of the stuff. It's soup for crying out loud. During the purchase I couldn't help but tell the cashier how excited I was about seeing Dani. "Now don't you go falling in love too soon young man" she said whilst scanning my tomato and basil soup and haemorrhoid cream that I'd picked up by mistake. The purchase came to £127. I was gobsmacked. I remember when I used to go into a newsagent with one coin, and leave with two bags of crisps, a chocolate bar, a can of coke, a magazine, and a few shelves. Nowadays there's CCTV everywhere! As I turned the corner, I saw Kathy and her boyfriend approaching, so I immediately buried myself in a huge pile of onions and waited for seven hours to ensure they didn't see me. When the over night staff found be asleep in the bulbs, I headed home and filled the bath tub with soup, dived in, and drank as much as I possibly could before bed. I simply had to feel better within two days of my departure, or I wouldn't have been able to go. I was too young to give up on true love, and too old to leave myself outside a Police station pretending to be an unwanted baby.

After a couple of days in bed, and few more bath tubs of soup, I became more able bodied, and managed to get out of bed and stand up without the help of the golf club I'd been using. Dani was worried I wouldn't be able to make it and I was determined to prove her wrong. I was permitted to work from home on that day, which gave me time to pack. People who claim that working from home is easy, have obviously never tried balancing a laptop on their knees whilst taking a bath full of soup before. I enjoyed my job, and it had huge potential for me to work my way up the ladder, but I also wanted to be reunited with Dani, and live a life of happiness together. I never wanted to go back to square one with either my job or Dani as I felt that job hunting was very much like dating, because you kept putting yourself out there, and kept getting rejected, until one lucky day, you finally just die. After a stressful journey, I'd made it to Ghana, and once corrupt public servants had denied my legitimate visa and demanded a back hander to allow me entry to the Country, I finally walked through customs and into the arms of Dani. It was so great to see her. I didn't want to put her down. She introduced me to her housemate 'Chabuddy Najib', and before we went back to their house, we went out for a drink at a club Dani had discovered. Her house mate was a nice man, and not the sex attacker I had imagined him to be. Dani introduced me to her new local friends, and whilst they were all incredibly freaky and unreasonably dull degenerates besides Chabuddy Najib, I knew when to keep my mouth shut, as the last time I opened it to express an opinion, a bee flew in and went down my thorax. Lesson learned.

Dani and I had a wonderful time together that evening. I was so pleased to see her, as was she with me, and eventually the muppets left us to it with Chabuddy Najib. We went back to where I would be staying with her, and as she pointed it out from the car window, I asked her if a plane had recently hit the building. The architecture was very different to what I was used to in the UK and India for that matter. Once Dani assured me the building was structurally sound, I unpacked a few things, then rattled her into the next day. Dani was nothing like my ex who had weird fetish for dressing up in her own clothes and pretending to be faithful. Whilst it was a great start to the trip in terms of Dani, I was still apprehensive about living in an abandoned warehouse surrounded by creepy people. I hadn't landed until late on my first day, so with it being dark, I hadn't yet experienced Ghana in daylight, and I had another five days to get to like it. On my first full day in Ghana, I went for breakfast at a local café with Dani and Chabuddy Najib. Luckily, I'd bought a loaf of bread at Heathrow, as I wouldn't have fed the food here to rabid dogs. I showed willing by placing a spoonful of whatever it was into my mouth, then keeping it between my cheeks and pretended I needed the toilet, in order to throw up what tasted like a cross between window cleaner and arm pits. If Dani and I didn't get on this week, at least I'd lose enough weight to reach my goal of a three-inch waist. Excited and starving, I went to the beach with Dani. We frolicked between lumps of turds in the sea, shared a few beers at a beach bar, and laid on the sand chatting and kissing.

Dani placed her hands on my cheeks, and then on my face, looked me dead in the eyes and said, "all I've ever wanted is a man with perfect skin and hair and teeth and body proportions and endless supplies of money and intelligence, but I am willing to forget all that and settle for you". A tear left my right eye. I replied "same". I wasn't sure if I was experiencing genuine emotion, or whether the box of onions I had sat in the week before had taken longer than expected to kick in. I took her and Chabuddy Najib for dinner that evening, then drilled Dani into the wall later that evening. I wasn't sure whether I was liking Ghana or not, as my thoughts and emotions were all Dani based, and hadn't had time to enjoy the Country itself. It was ok, but nothing special. Although I was only on my second day in Ghana, Dani had asked me on several occasions if I would move out to Ghana to live her, and I began seriously doubting my own brain to consider it. The next day we relaxed, drank wine by a pool, had an amazing time, and planned for us to meet her misshaped friends at a club that evening with Chabuddy Najib, who by now I really liked and would have contemplated acting like I knew him if he was in England. Little did I know, Dani had been dating a Lebanese friend of Chabuddy Najib when she first got here for a few days but dumped him because he was violent and hit her. I was outraged, and probably wouldn't have flown out to Ghana if I had known this prior. I did find it strange why she called me out of the blue a week into moving out to Ghana, and now it made sense. I could only appreciate her honesty, as the lanky streak of piss that hit her was going to be at the club, we were attending that evening. Dani apologised for not telling me about him, and the only way I'd get through the forthcoming evening was in the only way I knew how to. Lots of Whiskey and brutal murder. If anybody reading this suffers from feelings and stuff, alcohol may also be the answer for you. You do not need to consult your doctor about this, just do it, trust me. The same friends that used to pressure me into taking drugs and alcohol then bullied me later in life into drinking kale smoothies and attending Army boot camp. Life was confusing and hard!

Dani, Chabuddy Najib and I arrived at the run-down garden shed we had planned to attend that evening, grabbed ourselves a drink, and danced to horrendous music I hated. I prayed that Dani's ex would not turn up, then a hideously unattractive bag of puss bowled over to her. It was Abdel the asshole, her ex. This was the second worse news I'd received after adopting a snow leopard in 2013 and transpired the leopard wasn't allowed to live with me at the Playboy Mansion, so my leopard themed guest bedroom looked ridiculous and was a waste of money. Dani brought Abdel the asshole over to me and introduced me as her 'friend' then wandered off to find Chabuddy Najib. That instantly wound me up. I explained to Abdel the asshole that Dani and I we're at the start of a faithful relationship of true love and that if he ruined it for us, I would set him on fire and repeatedly punch him in the face whilst he was burning to death. Dani retuned, gave me a hug in front of Abdel the asshole, and said "you are one in a million babe". Whilst her words were well received, I struggled to forget the fact that this meant there were approximately seven thousand eight hundred and twenty-eight other people just like me in this world. It was not a compliment after all.

Abdel tensed his scrawny muscles to try and impress Dani and intimidate me. His arms were like bent cotton buds and little did he know, I regularly heated food in the microwave that had 'oven cook only' written on the packaging, so I knew I was significantly harder than that parasitical dweeb. I could see by the twinkle in Dani's eyes that she was not over the deformed rat. The remainder of the evening went ok but not great, and we left the run down shed to get a McDonalds. I didn't order a happy meal, as any meal can be a happy meal if you drink enough vodka and deny that your problems exist. Dani was very quiet on the way home. I wondered if I was wasting my time treating her like an iPhone 5, when she treated me like a Nokia 3210. Dani and Chabuddy Najib wanted to go onto another club, and I wasn't in the right frame of mind. Dani jokingly said, "come on, go big, or go home", seriously underestimating my willingness to go home. The three of us did go on to another club, and Dani spent the evening flirting with every male in sight but me.

The following day was my last in Ghana. Dani had no longer mentioned the prospect of me moving out there with her and was an uneventful last day. Every time I went to cuddle Dani, she shouldered me, and was weak as I hadn't eaten for five days. Chabuddy Najib gave me a lift to the airport after a non-existent goodbye with Dani, and I couldn't wait to leave the Country. I checked in my suitcase and then spilled a banana milkshake down my black jeans. I was wrathful. I went into a trendy clothes store and the hot sales lady asked me what size waist I was looking for on my new jeans. I got flustered and, in an attempt, to impress her, I went in a few inches lower to look cool and trim and then ended up hiding in the changing room in agony, waiting for her shift to end because I couldn't get them on properly or off. I paid for the jeans and left the store with them half on, and thankfully I managed to catch my flight. I was riddled with anxiety and bored stiff on the plane. You wouldn't think it was possible to play 'Twister' by yourself in the aisle, but loneliness and vodka breeds ingenuity apparently. Dani and I had to be over, and all I could think about was the six stages of a conventional break up. Sadness, anger, try and sleep with her friends, send her a million giant deadly hornets in a birthday card, kill her, and finally acceptance. I landed safely back in London, and zoomed home to cook my favourite meal. I tried taking a photo of my dinner to upload on social media, but the Haribo bears wouldn't sit up properly. My debit card had also been skimmed in Ghana, so I had to pray for the scammer who had probably invested a lot of time on trying to defraud me, only to discover that I had eight pence available for withdrawal.

CHAPTER 15 – MEGA SUPER WHORE

Summer was on the horizon and was my favourite season of the year. I loved all the short skirts and low-cut tops, but they did make me look a bit homosexual. I needed to get beach body ready and put myself out selling myself. The average Great British summer only lasted thirty-five minutes and I had to be ready to find a tiny patch of grass next to some dog excrement and don a thong before it rained again. I started small by joining a fitness page on social media then logged off and ordered a kebab. Within a week I'd nearly completed five whole press ups. I needed a healthy body to sustain a healthy mind and made sure I had a lot going on to keep me distracted.

I was DJ'ing, work was busy, I purchased a treadmill, and I remembered I was still 'it' from a game of 'Tag-your it' in 1988 and spent night after night trying to track the individual down on the internet in order to tag them back. I couldn't stand unfinished business. After a week of my return from Ghana, I got an unexpected call from Dani. She was in tears and said she had really missed me since I had gone. She must have been dumped by whoever followed me. Dani was again honest with me and told me that on the night I left Ghana she accidently slept with four men, but regretted it, and wanted to move back to England to be with me. I assumed she was pulling my leg, but she came home to live with her parents a few days later and contacted me to meet up and get back together, and I couldn't have been happier. Arsenal said I was being trampled over and that I should check Dani didn't have any sexual diseases or was pregnant. It did make me worry I was a mug and a potential cash cow if this were the case. The most important thing to me was that Dani back home and we were potentially getting back together. Dani did not have a job for the short term, and so I knew that to keep her interested, I would need a lot of money to take her out and help support her financially until she started a new job. Or she had a baby. I researched the best loan repayments on-line, then very quickly decided to plan an ostentatious heist instead. I scraped together my last few pennies from my pot and took Dani for a romantic can of cider and a petrol station pork pie at the local park. We immediately got back together, and I told her I would get money. Dani always said that money cannot buy happiness, but it's more comfortable to cry in a Mercedes than on public transport.

Dani was not a gold digger and gave me an hour to come up with nine thousand pounds in untraceable bank notes. I told Dani how I was planning to commit a heist and that if all went well, we could go on holiday to literally anywhere in the World but Ghana. Dani remained firm that I mustn't consider the heist unless I could guarantee getting her the money without bringing her name into disrepute. I had a Goldfish that could break dance on the carpet, but only for twenty seconds, and only once, so I uploaded the video I had made to social media with a view to becoming an overnight millionaire, but only person viewed it, and that was me. I had high hopes that the video would become my retirement plan. I had run out of all plausible options to increase my financial status, and therefore a heist was the last chance saloon for me.

I laid in bed that evening thinking about the perfect heist. All I needed was a team or ruthless criminals, guns, a disguise, an alibi, lots of money, and a plan to make it happen. I'd seen many films involving bank jobs, and they always use this list of things, but never got away with it, so I had to think outside the box. In the end I decided to go into the bank alone, dressed as a cartoon burglar with the black eye mask, black and white striped jumper, a fake moustache, black bobble hat, and a huge bag that said 'swag' on the side. I ran up the counter holding a full-grown Emperor penguin that I had got drunk before I went in and threw it at the first clerk to confuse her. Then I pulled out a fake stick of animated dynamite and demanded all the cash whilst insisting that another clerk get some bolt cutters and removed the chains from all the tiny pens. I set off the fire sprinklers, braided a customer's hair, and then filled my swag bag with hard cash. Everyone was so confused by the sequence of events that happened, they hadn't had time to comprehend it, let alone think about phoning the Police.

The drunk penguin went insane, so I slipped past it and out into the street completely undetected. I jumped on a bus, and the driver let me on without accepting any payment from me. I knew the costume was a magical idea. I got off the bus, then into my first getaway car. I drove to Manchester, then switched cars again. I drove to Brazil, then switched cars again. I switched to a motorbike and rode to my next-door neighbour's house. I then called a taxi to take me home. I emptied the swag bag over my bedroom floor, and I had more cash than I'd ever had before. Well in excess of eight pence. I had gotten away with the most impossible crime of the millennium, and the general public rated me as highly as other myths such as the Loch Ness monster, dragons, UFO's, being sober, and not getting lost in Ikea. I bought Dani a giraffe from the proceeds. I was aware that she lived on the fortieth floor of a tower block and had no garden, and hated giraffes, but it was a token of my appreciation, and I knew she would love it. I had already reviewed her tenancy agreement, and it only referred to having no cats or dogs on the premises. There was absolutely no mention of giraffes, so it was going to be a gift to remember.

For the next couple of months, I wined and dined Dani at all high-profile restaurants and events she wished to attend, until the money was almost all gone. On the last night of money, I took Dani to the casino and blew the remainder of my illegally obtained cash on roulette. I very much doubt that anything screams sexy more than me when I tilted a giant crisp bag into my mouth, and endlessly spilled more than half of them down my shirt whilst muffling "another two thousand quid on number twenty-nine mate". Dani spent most the evening on her phone texting other men. Casually minding my own business, I placed my head between her head and her typing hands, and viewed a text message from somebody called 'nine inch Liam from Putney' that read 'I cannot wait to have sex with you again tomorrow', to which Dani replied 'I am going to dump Jamie in the morning then head straight to yours so we can have years of border line illegal porno sex'. Dani pulled her phone away and I asked her if she was going to dump me and sleep with somebody else. She made out I was dyslexic, and that the message was from Basildon Council chasing up the remainder of her overdue Council tax. I had been such an idiot reading it wrong and jumping to conclusions. I believed her version in a flash, then slid hundreds of notes into a fruit machine. Dani and I drank washing up bowls full of champagne, then with only a few scraps left from my bottomless swag bag, we picked up the loose change and went to do a weekly food shop. The best thing about drunken food shopping, was waking up the next day and wondering what type of cake I had for breakfast, and if my girlfriend was going to have sex with a bloke called Liam. Dani had stayed at mine on the night of the casino, and when we awoke in the morning, I rolled over to kiss her, and she jumped out of my bed lightning fast to get into the shower.

I continued to lay in bed and watched videos on my phone of hamsters in waist coats tap dancing. I'd seen them all before but was never a bad idea to watch them all again. Dani's phone was constantly beeping and nine inch Liam from Putney had texted her things like 'have you dumped Jamie yet?', 'are you pregnant with my baby or not?' and 'had another sex role play idea for us to try today when were wearing our '#Liam&Dani4Life' T shirts and you delete all your photo's of you and Jamie as I pull out of you. Don't forget to wax your minge' etc. Dani came out the bathroom and I pretended I'd never seen her phone and went one further to playing it cool by pretending I didn't know what a phone was. Dani started plastering herself in make up and perfume then put her shoes on and packed up all her belongings. "Are you going somewhere babe?" I asked. "I forgot to tell you, but you're dumped, and I am going to meet one of my boyfriend's today for a much better time with him than I ever did with you whilst totally naked" she replied, then rushed out of my front door. I was usually rather good at deciphering code, however something felt wrong this time. I went back to sleep for an hour, and when I awoke, I scrolled through social media, and learned that Dani was in a relationship with a someone called Liam, and she had uploaded a photo of them both naked on the bouncy castle making love. I had not seen it coming. I spent the evening crying into two kebabs and another one.

CHAPTER 16 – HELPING A FELLOW LOSER

On my way to the train station for work the next day, I was upset, and everything annoyed me more than usual. My toilet was blocked which lead to me running late intern commenced the anger. The 'International loudest and most annoying repeat sneeze' competition was being held on the seat next to me, and I didn't mean to generalise, but I witnessed a gang of ladies saying "Ugh why is my handbag so heavy?", then sat down, have a rummage through it, and we're all "ok, keys, purse, book, sandwich, phone, water, make up, anvil, other sandwich, a baby, back up anvil, surf board, staircase, yup I definitely need all this stuff". I was about to flip and took some deep breaths in a bid to calm myself down.

I overheard two ladies in the seats behind me discussing how a creepy man that was listening in to their conversation, but I thought forty-eight-year Julia from Eastwood who was having a knee operation on the sixteenth of October was right, as some blokes are weird. I arrived in London and headed into the office and my unusual behaviour was noticeable. Arsenal had emailed me from the other side of the desk to see if I wanted to nip out for a tea to chat about it, but I was oblivious to my surroundings as I hadn't had my breakfast Red Bull yet. I went into the works kitchen and cursed a thousand times over. We could send people to the moon but couldn't invent a vending machine that accepted slightly wrinkled £5 notes. I put my leg through the glass screen and crawled back to my desk. My boss pulled me to one side to discuss my behaviour, and I told him about Dani. News travelled fast to the rest of the team, and they comforted me with comments such as 'told you she would', 'she looked like a dirty one', and 'me and my mates all had a go on her, but she was average at best'. My boss let me leave early as I was in no position to function on my job properly, and my leg didn't stop bleeding, so I headed out to get a few bits before heading home. Upon exiting a hardware store, I saw Kathy with her boyfriend looking at large expensive engagement rings in a jeweller's window, and I casually walked past whistling with a fifty percent off toilet brush in my carrier bag, so we both knew who was winning at life. I got home, placed a few plasters on my leg, and entered what I had eaten and drank over the last two days into my fitness app. This resulted in an ambulance being sent to my house, which was ideal, as they fixed my leg properly. I still had not heard from Dani, but that was probably due to me having accidentally left my phone on my desk, and then I realised how it must have felt for parents who lose their babies in shopping centres.

Having been in this position on multiple accounts before, I drew on my previous experiences to help myself heal. As none of my ideas had ever worked, I decided to try something brand new by getting an appointment with a sleep hypnosis councillor. Arsenal found me a lady with her own clinic in Colchester and I went on my not so merry way to get cured. The councillor was lovely lady with a softly spoken and calming voice. I laid back on the special chair for people that were clueless about life, closed my eyes, and she spoke affirmations and words of assistance at me for an hour. I was totally relaxed, and my mind had drifted allowing me to temporarily forget Dani. When the lady told me to open my eyes at the end of the session, I felt on top of the world for the next hour. If I could perform this technique twelve times a day, I had a chance of mental survival. When I got home, I listened to the recording she had made for me at the session, and again I went into a hypnotic state of bliss. I then got into my car and played her CD recording whilst on the motorway and swerved over the cat eyes and into the back of a Waitrose lorry. I awoke upside down and halfway up a tree. The Police weren't sympathetic to my cause and advised me that driving at 95mph with my eyes closed in a deep hypnotic state could be considered dangerous. What the f*** would they know?

My day of sleep hypnosis was at a sudden end, so I tried the gym again. I did twenty minutes on the treadmill, ten minutes on the defibrillator, and four days in hospital. I couldn't live like that, and then a conversation at work caught my attention. A lady on my team was discussing medium readers. She was a particularly sceptical person like me and said she had seen around fifty medium readers and they were all phonies that lacked any high-level detail, and simply made it up as they went along, however one of them blew her away with details nobody else could have known. Having spooked me, my ears pricked up and I caught the person in questions name and location, then researched them for hours. I located the lady in question at a property on Canvey Island and booked in to see her. I'd never done anything like this before and was excited yet apprehensive, safe in the knowledge that my sceptical work colleague was no pushover and wouldn't have given this lady praise if she didn't mean it. I was done with dealing with problems and had this one last hope of guidance to look forward to. I never ran away from my problems, I would always lay on the sofa, drink lots of whiskey, and then drunkenly update my social media page with a dangerously hungry and attention seeking, yet coded status, just like real man do. Now I had one last chance to fix myself.

On the day of my appointment with the medium reader I felt a little better within myself. I skipped out of my front door, and noticed a new neighbour moving in. I said hello, and they gave me a plant by way of an introduction. It was a lovely gesture, considering I should have been buying them a moving in present, but I couldn't keep stuff alive. I was only just hanging in there by the skin of my teeth myself. I gave it back to them and proceeded to my destination. I signed in at the medium readers work place and sat in the reception area awaiting my reading. A man sat next to me and we began chatting as we waited patiently for our readings. He told me that he and his wife had divorced, and he was struggling to cope, he wanted her back, and sought some guidance from above, sparking up a meeting of the great minds. It was obvious that the poor man had it even worse than me, so I decided not to burden him with the true purpose for my reading. I told him that I went to Ikea for some impulse purchasing and got lost for three hours leading to me to take a nap in a showroom bed. As it was hot in there, and I only ever sleep naked, I explained how I was arrested when a school trip walked past and reported me to security, and therefore needed some after life reassurance with reference to shopping online. He asked me for relationship advice, so clearly, he was either unbalanced or desperate. I confirmed that if he sent her a text, then after six years she still hadn't replied to him, it was a good sign, because she was obviously still thinking about it. I'm proud that my past experiences and intricate wisdom could be filtered down to the next generation.

The medium reader came to meet me in reception. No matter how many stupid things I kept doing in my life, I always remembered that Little Red Riding Hood couldn't figure out that a talking wolf in drag wasn't her grandmother, and then I felt a bit better. This reading was a good idea and made me feel better. She was a friendly Scottish lady in her late 50's with a wide smile named Grace. I followed her to the place of waiting ghosts, and I sat down ready to be educated. She could sense my resistance straight away and asked me to calm down to let the spirit world in, otherwise the next thirty minutes would be a waste of both our time. Grace began receiving data from the dead and relaying some information back to me. She started a little too vague for my liking, and I still wasn't sure if she was the real deal or not, when suddenly things ramped up. Grace was nailing everything and telling me things about me that nobody else could possibly know. She even knew about the super fun game I play alone when I turn the shower off but refuse to leave the bath tub because my feet were not allowed to touch the tiles until I was dried off and fully dressed, and the secret picture I had from an adult magazine with Kathy's face glued over the top of Linda Lusardi 's face that I kept in a safe behind four boxes labelled 'seriously boring work stuff'. Grace was without question a fully-fledged psychic. She claimed to have my great grandmother with her and told me her name. I didn't even know her name, as I was very young when she died and always knew her as 'nanna'. I had to verify this with family but turned out to be true. When Grace told me that Kathy and Dani had been seeing people behind my back for some time when I was dating them, their names, the names of the people they were cheating on me with, and the GPS coordinates of where the sins took place, I had zero or less doubt that she was naturally gifted, and could see why my work colleague rated her so highly. Grace then offered me some words of wisdom from my ancestors that saw and we're still seeing everything and up there trying to protect me. This lady was worth every penny. Grace advised me that my Great Grandad wanted me never to get any more tattoos on my face, and that Lisa War had recently killed someone when she accidently sprinted head on into into a speeding lorry. Apparently, Lisa had to drag the driver out of the vehicle to offer mouth to mouth although it was already too late. I appreciated that it was mind blowing to know we lived on a 4.5 billion-year-old rock that travelled at 67,000 MPH through space, but still, I'd rumbled my ex's in half an hour for £60, and that was the best thing ever.

My meeting with Grace had given me some form of closure. Of course, it was not gratifying to hear what I had always suspected, nevertheless the session had answered what I needed to know, and even offered words of comfort and advice to allow me to move on to bigger and better things. I wanted to be famous, so that was my new focus. The youth of today have it so easy when it comes to being famous. Just set up a free social media profile and lie about being a model or create a free video sharing account and claim you have a channel. When I was younger you had to work hard to be captured on VHS falling from a tall cliff and bouncing off jagged rocks into a deep well half full of acid. If you didn't die, you were rewarded with five seconds of fame on the TV and your parents got £250 from Jeremy Beadle. I ran my idea about becoming famous past Jamarn, Jamie Pantsoff, Ribena Cortina, and Arsenal, and they all laughed. They said I needed to have a talent, an acting capability, an idea, or possess some sort or guru status to pass onto others, bla bla bla. I angled an entire honey roast hair sandwich into my awaiting gob and jumped on line to investigate further.

Nothing jumped out at me, so I flew to the Netherlands to spend an afternoon eating hallucinogenic magic mushrooms. I learned that there were one hundred and sixty-five canals in Amsterdam and one hundred percent of them smelled of boiled cabbage. A kind passer-by told me that I didn't have an eight-metre-wide light bulb screwed into my bottom, and therefore I could sit down safely without it smashing. I sat down and suddenly had two psychedelic induced visions prior to vomiting again. The first was to open a suitcase shop at the airport. I'd never seen anybody at an airport with their arms full of clothes realising they had forgotten to pack their suitcase, but it didn't mean there wasn't a gap in the market for it. Low and behold, somebody must have tapped into my brain, stolen the idea, then gone back in time to start this new venture, as there was already a company doing so. Crafty buggers. My second brain wave had to show more promise, otherwise I would die a non-famous failure, and go directly to hell, where more than one person waits until the last minute of a boring team meeting to raise their hand for one more quick question. I was bilious of cyclists that thought traffic lights displaying red did not apply to them and those who selfishly rode in the middle of the road thinking they were competing in the tour de France, when they we're just mighty ignorant tarmac hogging dolts. If I could legally rewrite the highway code to have cyclists omitted from our roads, less people would be sullen, and I would become a hero. I scratched my brain thinking about trap doors on a timer at traffic lights and introducing minimum speed limits with lengthy prison sentences for those who didn't adhere to the strict rules under my new laws. I planned to bring back the death penalty for people that refused to use their indicators when required and cancelling BMW drivers. This was hands down the best idea I'd ever had.

I was going to improve so many peoples when my re-written

highway code was legislated. Journey times would be improved and less painful for motorists. I would become a national icon and make huge amounts of money and Holly Willoughby would fire herself at me. I ran out of mushrooms, so I got drunk as quickly as I could to keep the momentum of my idea. Fortunately, I'd had ample experience in doing this. It's bizarre how drinking three cups of water a day often felt almost impossible yet hoovering up twelve pints of Tequila in half an hour always went down like an elephant on a seesaw. My creative juices we're flowing. Workmen would no longer be able to section off a fifty mile radius of a road for a year in order to repair an inch square pot hole, and people who waited for traffic lights to turn green first, before then starting their mirror signal and find first gear to manoeuvre routine would automatically be hauled out of their vehicles at gun point and ordered to rescind their driving licenses on the spot. Possibly killed. Christmas was only a month away, so if I could finish writing my new rules then rush the legislation through, I would have enough money to buy a helicopter. As it stood, if someone stole my identity, I would merely laugh at them, and mock them for now having no money and grey hair. I still had a half empty sag aloo tub in the back of my fridge which was so old, that when I attempted to open it, something closed it from the inside. I needed cash and fame faster than ever.

For the next few days I bunked off work and put my everything into changing the law twenty-three hours at a time. I was exhausted. I allowed myself a strict hour break per day to watch Thomas the Tank Engine and to sleep. After a few episodes, Thomas got me stressed. There was always some major drama on the tracks, and nothing ever went smoothly on that doomed island. They had derailed trains, cargo spills, broken trucks, an engine stuck in a tunnel, it was a bloody shamble. In the end I had to stop watching it as I put my TV through the living room window. At last my new highway code was complete. I was on the first step to fame and fortune. My days of nonstop hassle at work then rushing home to consume a few boxes of wine of an evening which ended with doing an impromptu conga, then realising I lived on your own, were about to be over.

I posted my proposed new laws to the Prime Minister, and went back to work, knowing I would only be there for no more than a few days until my legislation was passed in the houses of parliament. I was in the works kitchen and got into a conversation with Jamarn about how stressed I was. She offered to make me a cup of tea and said, "look mate, you just got to take it with a pinch of salt" and then wet herself. I thought she was giving me good advice, as she was a lovely caring lady, but instead my tea tasted horrendous.

After three days had passed without a response to my communication, I felt more than enough time had progressed to have my new rules implemented. I'd paced up and down for what felt like forever waiting for the postman to deliver yet more piles of recycling. My accountant told me I only had a month to live, so I decided to head over to ten Downing Street and apply some much-needed pressure. I couldn't face another single day of getting up for work with my only chirpy thought being 'oh well, only another forty-five years to go until retirement', to cheers me up. I turned into Downing street with every window on my car rolled down whilst blaring the most upfront clown step wobble drum and bass as loud as the car would allow without snapping into parts. I stopped directly outside number ten and switched off the engine. There was Policeman outside the building, who I had seen on the news years ago. He must have been hungry for a sit down to take the weight off his feet. I attempted to walk past the copper and ring the door bell, however I was stopped in my tracks, and grilled about the purpose of my visit and to provide identification. I squared him up and gently said "do you know who I am mate?". He looked puzzled and shook his head to denote he was oblivious to my existence. I proceeded with "just get Davo the pig poker out here now and he'll fill you in". Auspiciously, Mr Camera opened the front door, so I dropped the Police Officer on the pavement.

"I haven't received my money for the new highway code yet" I said. Mr Camera retreated inside and hurriedly locked the door before I could kick it off its hinges. Within seconds I heard the Officer on the floor radio for back up. "Code red nutter at the front of number ten", and a squad of people parachuted from a chinook and surrounded me. I was placed in handcuffs and made to eat dirt from the side of the road. Mr Camera came out with a can of petrol and a box of matches. I suspected he was going to make me a small fire to keep warm until the meat wagon arrived, but he threw my new highway code book on to the floor and burned it. As Mr Camera walked away, I told the Army that I hadn't done anything wrong, and that they should let me go, but they insisted I was caught on camera driving briefly in a bus lane back in 2005.

CHAPTER 17 – SARA AND THE NORTHERN TROLL

Mr Camera agreed to drop any charges against me concerning the harassment towards him outside his home, and besides Dani, nobody else knew about the Heist I carried out, nevertheless I was still sentenced to twenty nine years in prison because two of my cars wheels went marginally over the road markings and into a bus lane for a combined total of three metres outside the Ritz luxury hotel when I picked up Kathy one evening in London nine years previous. I'd have only got a month in prison if I had murdered a baby whilst posting something factual that contradicted the Government's official narrative on-line.

The UK judicial system had always been the laughing stock of Europe, as punishments were never comparable with the crimes committed, but this was a piss take even for them. The one rule for one and one for another rule to reach epic proportions this time, and said powers were acting in ultra vires. As I stood in the dock waiting for public servants to take me away, my mind had already began plotting a prison break. I was overwhelmed with fear about sharing a cell with a violent rapist allergic to not having sex, nicknamed 'Mr Enormous', who was four times my size and addicted to Viagra. I lost all common sense and made a rash decision to escape from Court there and then. I squeezed the rail in front of me to compose myself and leapt into the centre of the room. The jury we're screaming, and the Judge's wig fell off his head and fortuitously onto my head when he began shouting at me. It was carnage. The first thirty-two years of childhood are always the hardest, and I'd finished that portion of my life, ready to embark on an altogether alternative campaign. Security began closing in on me, so I took a member of the jury hostage in melancholy. I didn't want to bring anybody else down with me, but she was ridiculously sexy, and she had blown me a kiss during the trial because she thought I was a real criminal. I placed my arm tightly around her neck and dragged her outside the Court whilst whispering "I'm so sorry about this", to which she replied, "Its ok I love bad boys just please don't stab me too much".

I assured her I was not going to hurt her and trailed through with "well if you like bad boys, it may interest you to know that I once ate spaghetti whilst wearing a white T shirt". She orgasmed on the spot and asked, "will you marry me?". I had other things besides marriage to think about at that moment in time, so I told her I'd mull it over once we were safe from the armed units firing at us. We shook off the Police and security by running into an underground car park upon which I stole a car and told the hostage she was free to go. "I'm not going anywhere hubs" she replied. I'd spent my whole life looking for the perfect woman to no avail, yet the moment I abscond from court with a hostage to use as a human shield to protect me from the bullets and commit a robbery, Miss Right proposes to me. We both got in to the pilfered car and my potential fiancé took the wheel so I could evade detection by crouching down on the back seat. "I'm Sara Hashbrown and I'm waiting for an answer to my question" she said. I panicked that she may take me back to Court and hesitantly replied "Oh erm yeah er course I definitely want to marry you". Sara explained that she didn't do this with all the men she met, just the criminals, then called her Mum to book a day off work so they could go wedding dress shopping. Whilst telling Sara to break the speed limit and dodge the road block ahead, I asked her if she thought we we're rushing our relationship as I'd never had anybody that wanted to spend time with me without being paid to. She said, "not really" and carried on mowing down pedestrians like skittles. It was surreal for me, as I was used to stopping women in the street and saying "hey want to play a new fun cool game with me, all you have to do is hold my hand and cuddle me in public, then make love to me, and fool everyone into thinking we're an item forever by keep repeating it for life, it will be absolutely hilarious".

The Police had somehow tracked our stolen vehicle and began vigorously pursuing us. They we're hot on our bumper and Sara put her foot to the metal to create some distance. I scrambled around in the boot searching for something to break my handcuffs off with, and the owner of the vehicle must have been a bolt cutter salesperson, which was a slice of good luck, as I found a pair of bolt cutters. I wriggled free from my handcuffs and made a few calls for help. I rang Greg Fatcheese from Sara's mobile phone and asked him if I could borrow a car from his auto repair shop in Benfleet and lots of money right away. He was an hour into a psilocybin trip and agreed to help me. I guided Sara to Greg's workshop, and by the time we arrived, he was in an altered state of consciousness. He asked me if I liked one of his customers car's that he had removed the wheels and replaced with toilet seats. I was impressed, but the customer only dropped the car off to replace a faulty brake light. I told Greg it was jaw dropping but was very much working to a dead line. I grabbed the money, got into the new car, and told Sara to floor it to a marina down the road. The Police were nowhere to be seen or heard, so they had either given up on us, or heard a rumour that somebody had told somebody else online that they didn't agree with their exact opinion, and therefore authorised all Police forces in the Country to be deployed to pursue the person. Sara and I got to the marina to find all the boats had gone. The sea had been concreted over and turned into a whopping pop-up Wetherspoons. I was screwing. I noticed a small narrow channel of water that lead to Tunisia, so Sara suggested we sprinted to Argos and bought a canoe. I wish I'd have thought of that. It made me realise I wanted to marry her. Never again would I have to say "bad news ladies, I've already got my eyes on somebody who's not interested in me. Sorry!", whilst never losing sight of the wise words my Grandma told the medium reader to tell me, being 'always look both ways before crossing a woman'.

Argos had one canoe left in stock, so we paid for the item, then sat watching all the kettles and garden furniture slide down the conveyer belt. After thirty seconds, my large package found its way to the light. Something I was not used to hearing frequently. Sara and I grabbed the canoe and raced back to the old Marina. My ultimate lifelong dream was to take a stretched limo to a McDonalds drive thru, pay for the food at the first window, and collect it at the second window without moving the car, and yet now my destiny was to row to Tunisia with Sara. We bought a keg of limoncello, a bendy straw, and prawn sandwich each from the local shop, then plonked our canoe in the water. I thanked Sara for all her help and gave her the option to back out of the row ahead if she wanted to, but she was hell bent on coming with me. Whether she was planning on murdering me or not, I had a fiancé. I'd no longer Google 'dying alone' to find the first link was to my own social media profile. We took hold of our oars and started the arduous one thousand six hundred and sixty-eight-mile-long paddle to Tunisia in our canoe.

The first few minutes went well, but then we started drinking the Limoncello which slowed down our estimated time of arrival by twenty years. My arms started aching, so I sat back and played some electronic roulette on my phone whilst Sara took the pain for both of us and continued paddling. As we reached the English / French water border, we saw lots of immigration control boats and feared we would be captured, and I'd go to prison. Personnel on the boats waved at us, gave us large sums of free money, then offered to tow us wherever we wanted to go. We didn't want to mock this offer of assistance, but I said it how it was. "Is Tunisia too far?" I asked. The Captain of the first vessel replied, "hop aboard we'll have you there in no time". Sara and I climbed up the ladder and onto the ship to have dinner with the Captain and his Officers. I told the staff on board in confidence that we didn't have our passports with us, and the Captain chimed in with "who does?" and everybody roared with laughter and we continued eating and smiling. We reached Tunisia half a century ahead of schedule, and well fed. "If you want a lift back give us a call day or night" the Captain shouted over the deck as we waved him goodbye. He really was a charming man.

We had no idea what our plan would be once we had reached Tunisia, so we went with the flow, and used our free money from the Captain to check into the poshest hotel with the most Brits, and drink unlimited amounts of alcohol until our liver's gave way. I won the hotel's Halloween competition for scariest make up and costume, and I hadn't even dressed up for it. Sara and I decided to enjoy our first evening together, then sort out the being an escaped criminal on the run abroad thing the next day. We met a young couple from the North of England and chugged the most highly illegal drugs from bongs with them for a few days straight. They took photos of us all getting high and the lady said, "I'll post these on social media and tag you in unless you're a wanted criminal", to which I replied, "yes I am actually", and they split their sides open laughing so hard, although I'm not sure why. She was a blithering idiot, but I wish I had her confidence to dare upload an unfiltered first attempt photo as her profile picture. I would have liked this couple a lot more if they weren't with us.

Sara and I had been solid drinking for four days straight, so we left early to get some sleep. I must have been getting old. We made amazing love and Sara told me that the sex was great, but she faked the cuddle. I collapsed on our panda skin divan at the penthouse and began snoring. I awoke a few hours later with a sharp pain in my head, partially blind, with little to no coordination between my brain and body apparent. I glanced around the room and Sara was nowhere to be seen. I checked the bathroom and she wasn't there either, but the skid marks on the pan were still fresh. The most rational explanation was that she had gone to get us some more alcohol or met a financial advisor to discuss our joint pension. Then alarm bells rang when I noticed the canoe was missing. Upon further inspection I discovered her clothes and prawn sandwich were missing too. She must have left me. I was about to become the best new single on iTunes this week and be forced to write "I've killed before and I'll kill again", in my internet dating profile to really weeds out the players. I peered out of the window to observe a dozen or so Tunisian Police Officers running towards my room with the Northern couple we had been drinking with the past few days.

I located a dressing gown and a shower cap in the wardrobe, so I placed them on, grabbed my bendy straw and money, and made my way casually out of the hotel. As I turned around, I saw a Police helicopter hovering an inch above the roof of our penthouse. David Camera leaned out of the sliding door with a megaphone and yelled "we know you are in there Jamie and we don't take bus lane offences lightly". I picked up some pace and scrambled to find the exit. There were Police everywhere, and a tank pulled up outside the front of the hotel. I dashed into another direction and saw Sara snogging the pushy salesman that tried flogging us monstrous tat for extortionate money on the first day. I knew it was her as she only had one pair of clothes and a canoe between her feet. I didn't want to jump to conclusions, but the signs were there with this one. I delicately removed the canoe from between Sara's feet whilst she was busy cheating on me, and filled with emotional hurt, I bolted towards a side gate. Sara clocked me and gave chase, and I foolishly stopped to hear her out. "What you just saw was an accident I wasn't cheating I just slipped on a dry spot and into that man and both our clothes fell off and lips became locked for twenty minutes when the air con came on" Sara explained. "Easily done I suppose" I replied, having been irrefutably convinced by her unthinkable story. We held hands and skipped out of the resort when the helicopter started circling the grounds. We made it to the coast and began hysterically paddling.

The sound of a helicopter grew closer and closer and Sara I and I paddled for our lives. David Camera arrived above our canoe and used a fishing rod to cast out a copy of my bus lane fine. "This will never go away Jamie" he bleated through his megaphone. The colossal wind from the helicopter and the strong choppy waters meant Sara and I were struggling on our 23kg death trap. The helicopter continued to decrease in altitude and came so close to us that I could smell bacon on Mr Camera's breath. The unavoidable happened, and our canoe capsized into one hundred feet deep freezing water. Sara and I we're sucked under by the current and David Camera scooped our canoe out of the water and flew away doing a deep booming laugh into his megaphone which echoed across the sea. I clawed my way up to the surface and took some deep breaths. I could not find Sara anywhere. I plunged back down into the water and took a short swim to find her, but Sara was nowhere to be found. Even she couldn't have been cheating on me this soon given our immediate environment. We were a few miles from the closest land, and I was rapidly losing body heat. I thought it would be a terrific idea to send a fax for help, but then remembered I didn't have electricity or fax machine. I was in a spot of cold bother and feared these we're my final few minutes alive.

CHAPTER 18 – TO WEE OR NOT TO WEE

As my life flashed before me, a lost goldfish the size of a boat that super speedily adapted to breathing sea water swam by. I grabbed its fin and it took me to the nearest land. I was safe, but Sara had to have been dead by now, and her blood was on our Government's hands. The Captain of the ship that took us to Tunisia heard about the kerfuffle on the Police scanner and came to collect me. We took the ship around the area of the incident to look for Sara, but all efforts failed. The Captain agreed to take me back to the France/England water border to await my connecting ferry.

I was honest with the Captain by telling him I was a wanted felon, but he said he was used to it and whipped out Snakes and Ladders from under the table. I had a cup of tea, shivered myself dry, won a few games of Snakes and Ladders, and headed back to England for Christmas. The Captain gave me a fake moustache to help evade authorities upon my return, and I caught my connecting ferry to Dover. I told passport control I'd lost my passport and they let me through. I called Greg Fatcheese to pick me up, and he drove high for eight two miles down the wrong side of the motorway to collect me. I told Greg about Sara and he said it was about time I had some good luck. It was great to be home.

My Mum agreed to let me hide at her house for a few decades and spent Christmas with her and my siblings and her new husband she had forgotten to tell me about. I bought everybody perfectly square presents, so they were easier to wrap and gave me months free to do other things. I wanted to buy Mum something sentimental to let her know how much I loved her, but I couldn't find anything square, so I opted for a sixteen feet tall ceramic dinosaur soup holder in a cardboard box. If that didn't say what I wanted to express, then nothing would. I purchased my siblings gift cards, as it was the best way to say, 'I was too lazy to think of a good gift to get you and I suspect you'd buy drugs if I give you cash'. We had a splendid Christmas day, and nobody died. I couldn't update my social media status, as I would have been captured and re-arrested, but I did scroll through and note Sara was now engaged to the Captain of the ship that saved us. It made my day when I lied to myself, and hoped I'd meet another unfaithful or unhinged stalker soon.

With Christmas out the way for another year, I had to wait three weeks until the next John Lewis Christmas advert was released and peddled into my eyes every fifteen minutes. I wasn't due back at work for a few more days, therefore decided to get my Mum some shopping before catching up on some long overdue sleep. Mum gave me list of things to purchase, so I headed to the supermarket. A pregnant lady in front of me at the fish counter was asked by a stranger in the queue "do you know what you are having?", and she replied, "I don't know, probably half a dozen smoked eel fillets". I alerted her to the fact that her response was exemplary, and she replied, "thanks have a nice day". I said, "have a nice baby", and chuckled all the way to the freezer section. I couldn't find one of items on my Mum's list anywhere, so I asked the manager of the supermarket to write me a note explaining to my Mum that I did genuinely look everywhere for the ice cream she wanted, but that they didn't have it. This intern knocked hours off the argument when I get home. Once home and mentally drained, I retired to my bed. I began wondering how my Nan and Granddad lived so happily together their entire lives and put it down to a direct result of them not having the technology to text 'what are you doing?', 'where are you?', and 'why are you ignoring me?' every twenty seconds. Slowly but surely, I began drifting off to sleep. My mind finally shut down and took me beyond the fifth stage of sleep. My brain seemed foggy and I was in a very deep state of unconsciousness. I felt my soul become separated from my physical body, and I could see myself down below, but I wasn't in my bed and I appeared to look younger. I hoped I'd died so that I could repeatedly haunt all my exes for their wrong doings until they joined me.

I heard a snapping sound like fingers clicking and felt myself returning to my body. A loud clap passed by my ears and I woke up in shock. I was discombobulated as to my whereabouts. I was sat in a leather chair in an unknown room, and a man opposite me asked if I knew where I was. I advised the man I didn't know where I was or what I was doing there. He informed me that he was a physiological therapist, and that under my Mum's instructions, I was undergoing specialist treatment to prevent me from wetting the bed. The man went on to say that in the first case he had ever seen in his forty years as a doctor, he witnessed me slip into an unknown state of linear regression during the process. I had revisited my previous life in a parallel universe which would replicate exactly and determine my future in this life without alteration. I was seven years old, the year was 2085, and I had wet pants on. My worst nightmare had come true. I had been reincarnated as myself!

The End.

ABOUT THE AUTHOR

I, Jamie Greenlees, have been involved with crass parody in one form or another since I can remember. I am an old soul, and 'Curseanova' is my first self-published book, having written numerous satirical articles for 'Figure 8 media'. I currently work full time for a North American Insurance Company, and despite the content of this book, I live happily with my girlfriend of five years now in South East Essex.

My favourite saying is 'morons take a knife and stab people in the back, whereas the wise take a knife, cut the cord, and set themselves free from the morons'. I listen to and DJ vinyl only jungle and drum and bass music. My pipeline dream is to have enough money to build a modern and self-sufficient off grid home in a remote part of the World, such as Alaska, and my best friend at work is whichever one brings cake and sausage rolls in to the office for sharing, which today was Brenda - I love that old trout. I am a firm believer that Zombies DO exist, having once looked at myself in the mirror before my breakfast Red Bull. Finally, I find it strange that when a cat licks its bottom people find it 'cute', yet when I do it, everybody on the train refers to me as a 'weirdo'.

CREDITS:

Becks G; For believing in my concept and supporting me. Thank you, Aurora.

Sheila Boakes; My charming Primary school teacher that recognised my warped imagination and championed my inspiration. You are truly a lovely lady.

Rik Mayall; Having grown up on The Young Ones, Kevin Turvey, Filthy Rich and Cat Flap, Bottom, Dangerous Brothers, The New Statesman, Comic Strip, Behind the Green Door etc, this legend never once wrote or performed in anything that wasn't brilliant. Rest in peace big man.

YouTube LisaHenderson1981; For encouraging me to go ahead and do something different.

My loud neighbours; I apologise for renaming my WiFi 'Noise Pollution Surveillance Van for Tyler and Mandy'. You looked utterly confused when twitching at the curtains, but you kept me entertained on the occasions I had writer's block, so cheers.

Worthy mentions; Greg Chapman, James Harris, Kunal Desai, Michael Bush, Charge908 family, Lucy Aimee Campbell, and anybody that knows me still crazy enough to buy my scribble. You're the tops.

Disclaimer: The person(s) portrayed in this book are **not** based on real people. Probably.

Free tip: Marry somebody who is a good cook. Looks will fade, but hunger won't. You're welcome.

Click here for bonus footage OR search for 'Danny Shotfire the

Rubber Duck Killer Reformed Crimanal' for further stupidity.

Printed in Great Britain
by Amazon